ACCOUNTING FOR THE SELF, LOCATING THE BODY

Kael Reid

ACCOUNTING FOR THE SELF, LOCATING THE BODY

Stories of Queerness and Place

Queer and LGBT+ Studies

Collection editor

Patrick Thomsen

LPP

These stories are dedicated to all of us who are finding our way in this complex world. Our paths are precious and full of possibility.

First published in 2025 by Lived Places Publishing

British Library Cataloguing in Publication Data
A CIP record for this book is available from the British Library.

ISBN: 9781915734808 (pbk)
ISBN: 9781915734822 (ePDF)
ISBN: 9781915734815 (ePUB)

The right of Kael Reid to be identified as the Author of this work has been asserted by them in accordance with the Copyright, Design and Patents Act 1988.

Cover design by Fiachra McCarthy
Book design by Rachel Trolove of Twin Trail Design
Typeset by Newgen Publishing, UK

Lived Places Publishing
P.O. Box 1845
47 Echo Avenue
Miller Place, NY 11764

www.livedplacespublishing.com

Abstract

Kael Reid's stories, lyrics, and poems delve into the complexities of queer existence, exploring themes of relationality, embodiment, movement, and place. A white settler, lesbian singer-songwriter turned genderqueer researcher and educator, Reid reflects on their life journey from a farm in southwestern eastern Canada[1] to the mountains of western Canada[2] and back. Reid's narratives cover diverse experiences: a moment of reflection while cooking lunch over a fire in the woods as a youth, sexual assault, watching a lesbian docu-drama, drug abuse, waking up beside a woman for the first time, homophobic violence, an unplanned pregnancy, a past-life experience while hiking, singing with a musical companion in a run-down biker bar, finding love, and undergoing gender-affirming top surgery. Through these tales, Reid connects to the more-than-human world and captures the essence of being human.

Key words

Body, Flesh, Gender, Homophobia, Land, Lesbian, Love, Music, Teaching, Place, Sexuality, Song, Spirit, Relationships

Content warning

This book contains references to and descriptions of situations that some readers may find distressing, including:

conversations with expletives

queerphobia

sexism

sexuality

sexual assault

substance use and abuse

violence

Contents

Learning objectives   ix

Introduction: Building a queer lineage through storytelling   1

Chapter 1   Groundhog in the woodpile   3

Chapter 2   Science class, 1987   9

Chapter 3   Orange blouse, red lipstick   21

Chapter 4   Melissa's pub, 1989   23

Chapter 5   High   41

Chapter 6   Go Fish   61

Chapter 7   A revelation   67

Chapter 8   The night we watched *The Puppy Episode*   69

Chapter 9   Wildhorse Creek Road   91

Chapter 10   Heal myself (Reid, 2006)   113

Chapter 11   Truckdriver (Reid, 2009)   117

Chapter 12   The only dyke at the open mic (Reid, 2009)   121

Chapter 13   In this soul, in this body   125

Chapter 14   Crying holy (Reid, 2011)   133

Chapter 15   Lesbians and biker dudes   137

Chapter 16   Uncle Jim   145

Chapter 17   I whispered the word, "lesbian"   153

Chapter 18   Rape fantasy   **157**

Chapter 19   When I was a little boy (Reid, 2011)   **163**

Chapter 20   A story of leaving   **165**

Chapter 21   Her   **169**

Chapter 22   Something 'bout you and me (Reid, 2016)   **173**

Chapter 23   Somewhere in between   **175**

Chapter 24   Together   **183**

Chapter 25   For the land of Beaver Valley   **185**

Chapter 26   The summer afternoon   **195**

Chapter 27   Lying on a hill   **201**

Discussion questions and recommended projects   **203**

Notes   **206**

References   **207**

Recommended resources   **209**

Index   **211**

Learning objectives

1. Readers will develop an understanding of the diverse lived experiences, highlighting the intersections of identity, place, and self-discovery.

2. Readers will critically analyze how geographical and social environments impact the formation and expression of gender and sexual identities.

3. Readers will be able to connect personal narratives to broader theoretical and empirical research on LGBTQ+ issues, enhancing their comprehension of assigned research-based academic texts through real-life accounts.

4. Readers will explore the concept of intersectionality by examining how different aspects of identity (e.g., sexuality, gender, gender expression, race, class, connection to place, and socio-economic status) intersect and influence personal experiences and societal interactions.

5. Readers will cultivate empathy and perspective-building skills by engaging with intimate stories of struggle, resilience, and joy, fostering a deeper appreciation for the complexities of LGBTQ+ experiences.

6. Readers will apply theoretical frameworks and research findings to understand and analyze the personal stories presented, bridging the gap between academic knowledge and real-world experiences.

Introduction: Building a queer lineage through storytelling

When we want to make sense of who we are, we often look to our families to know and understand ourselves. We turn to our childhoods, and to the adults who raised us, to account for the ways we view and experience the world, to fit the puzzle pieces of our lives together, to find answers about who we are. We research family trees and trace ourselves back through the branches of our lineage to unearth the rhizomes of our heritage. We follow our bloodlines like roads that crisscross one another on a map, or like footpaths and trails through the forest of our ancestry. To become familiar with our lineage orients our bodies towards that lineage, locating us in the world. Knowing where and who we come from helps us decipher ourselves and anchors us to other bodies, stories, and lives.

But what happens if our *queer* identities, bodies, lives, and lineages cannot be traced? What if we cannot follow our queer identities back through a family line—if pieces of us cannot be pinpointed in the pedigrees of our heterosexual family members or accounted for by examining the history of a family that is cisgender? What if our queer stories have been overlooked, deliberately left out, not talked about, or erased by our family of origin and society—our bodies and lives shrouded in secrecy, shame, and fear?

And, what if these fragments could be pieced together one by one, by reading, witnessing, and resonating with the stories of queer others? What if words and imagery could fill in the blanks of one's queer life and become the scraps of fabric that, when stitched together, create a whole person—a rich, lived life? What if, through story and words, queer people could be brought together in community with others? What if, through story and words, we could be related to one another?

Then, through the sharing of our stories that run in our DNA, my queer loved ones and I—friends, partners, their friends, their partners—and perhaps even you and I, would be kin. Queer storytelling would be an act of constructing a lineage, building family relations, and expressing love. Queer storytelling would thread our narratives together and weave an archive of authored ancestry that we would share with one another, pass down to our descendants like an inheritance that binds us, and locate us in time and place. Queer storytelling would create a *queer* genealogy—our bloodline, our heritage, our collective history of kinship.

1
Groundhog in the woodpile

I trudge across the quiet, snowy field facing south towards the hardwood forest on the farm that my parents bought back in 1979, when I was 8 years old. Now, I am 13 years old. The bitter February afternoon wind stings my cheeks. A little knapsack is slung over my shoulder.

In the woods, I follow the imprint of tractor wheels in the snow to a plywood shack, grey and faded from the weather. When we first moved to the farm 6 years ago, my sisters, Lucy and Ava, and I decorated the shack so we could play there. Now, the shack looks abandoned.

Opening the door, I look inside. Three rickety wicker chairs and a small table sit in the middle of the floor. Two rough-hewn, 3-foot boards are nailed to the wall beside the door, providing a make-shift set of shelves. A rectangular piece of light blue cotton fabric with tiny sprigs of flowers, now threadbare and frayed, hangs over the cracked window with rusty thumbtacks. There is a short stack of mismatched plates and bowls on the shelf. A couple of framed pictures hang crookedly on one wall. The floor is rotted away in one corner. One of the hinges on the door is rusted and broken. It smells like rat piss and mouse shit. We never could keep the rodents out of there.

I close the door and turn around, tramping a few steps in the the snow towards a large old stump. I sit down and open my knapsack, pulling out a wad of newspaper, a few short pieces of kindling and two small wedges of chopped wood from the woodpile beside the stove in our kitchen, a small book of matches, a fork, a pair of metal tongs, a can opener, a thermos of hot chocolate, and a can of Libby's Brown Beans. I clear away the snow in front of me until a small fire pit encircled by rocks appears. Among the rocks, I stack pieces of kindling, one on top of the other, in the shape of a tiny log cabin, like I learned at summer church camp. Crumpled paper stuffed inside the middle of the cabin lights quickly, and smoke drifts up into the frosty air. Blowing on the flames, I add more kindling, then, a piece of wood.

Opening the can of brown beans, I tuck it beside the piece of wood in the coals. I lean back on the stump. The forest stands on guard around me. Sugar maple, green ash, and yellow birch trees reach skyward from the crusty snow, cold and hardened from the long winter months. I feel held by their presence.

I breathe in the quiet air, and the stillness envelops me. I relish being away from the house. Away from Lucy's many health issues. My father's frustration and demeaning comments. My mom's quest to understand what's wrong with my sister, how to help her—the doctors, hospital visits, medical and psycho-logical tests, psychiatrists in white coats—and how to keep it all together. My own guilt that I am not sick. That I, too, am irritated with her. That I'm embarrassed by her. That I can't save her.

Then, a soft, strained sound comes from the calloused logs that my father and I stacked a few hours ago. I cock my head to the side, trying to make out the sound, but there is only the sound of the crackling fire in front of me.

In a few days, my father and I will return for the logs. He will buck them up with his chainsaw, and I will toss the pieces onto the trailer attached to the tractor. Then, we'll drive back to the house, unload the firewood on the porch, and stack it in neatly arranged piles.

When I help my father around the farm, he is impressed with my strength and determination. I try to make up for the fact that he has three daughters. He never says it out loud, but I think he wants a son. Sometimes, he jokes that he's the only man in the house, that he's surrounded by girls, outnumbered. Mostly, I think he's okay with it, but sometimes, there's something in his voice, something that suggests he got the short end of the stick. That he's longing for something that would make his life complete. That he feels alone.

And I feel guilty that I'm a girl.

I am determined to be the son he never had. To be his right-hand boy and help him around the farm. I don't mind so much because it means I get to spend more time with him.

And, it feels good being boyish. It feels good being noticed. It feels good when he brags to my mom about how strong I am, what a good worker I am. After a morning of tossing hay bales into the barn, he proclaims proudly one afternoon over the lunch table, "Katy sure is robust!" Pride brims inside me.

I eat a forkful of brown beans from the can in the fire, the warm syrupy legumes soft and velvety in my mouth.

Again, I hear the strained sound coming from the pile of logs. I drop my fork into the can of beans and rise from my stump in the snow. Following my ear to the edge of the woodpile, I kneel beside the logs, listening. It's the sound of a small animal breathing. Wheezing, panting, and grasping at life in the darkness between the logs. There is an awkward rhythm to the breath and the soft sound of "kuh…kuh…kuh" with each mouthful of air. There is a pause too, between gasps; the thin space between holding on and letting go.

As I crouch in the snow, the sound moves into my body. Down past my throat, along my windpipe, and into my heart. I realize it is the laboured breathing of the groundhog my father had shot earlier that day. He's always on a mission to rid the farm of groundhogs because they dig large holes around the fields. Holes that could cause one of our horses to break a leg should their hoof land in one. Holes that could cause a tractor to get jammed in the ground and break an axle.

Once, I accompanied my father as he drove our pickup truck out into the fields of the farm, looking for groundhog holes. When he found one, he blocked it with tightly packed dirt. "The back door," he told me. Then, he located the front door of the burrow and fed a large hose down the hole that he attached to the tailpipe of the truck. He turned on the engine and gassed the unsuspecting groundhog family to death.

As I huddle there by the woodpile, listening to the dying ground-hog, rage and dread suddenly bubble up and melt together into fiery lava in my blood, searing the thin membranes of my veins. The dark, red sponge marrow in my bones screams inside of me and rushes up to my neck, spreading up across my face.

A sudden urge grips me. I want to tear the log pile apart with fierce, angry fingers. Rip through the timber to the huffing and gasping until I find her, trapped, terrified and small, her brown, coarse fur caked with blood, eyes brimming with fear. Reach past my fear, grasping her limp body.

If her yellow rodent teeth sank into my hand from panic, drawing blood, I would ignore the pain. I would pull her up out of the icy logs and clasp her to my heart inside my red plaid lumber jacket. I would stroke her body and hold her as she rattles and rasps and dies in my arms. At least, she would die with the warmth of my body. Not alone in a cold, hard, winter woodpile.

But, I don't do any of it.

Instead, I kneel in the crunchy, frigid snow, listening to her short, laboured breathing, and cry. Frozen in my loyalty to my father and his gun and the pickup truct with the gassing hose. Frozen in the fear that if I went against his actions and dug the ground-hog out of the woodpile to try and save her, I would have to face him and tell him what I did, knowing it wouldn't end well for the groundhog anyway. Frozen in the understanding that if I defied him and told him that I didn't like that he killed groundhogs, he would be angry and something bad might happen to me.

Like the time when Lucy was on a weekend pass from London Psychiatric Hospital. She was living there because she was sick in the mind and my parents didn't know how to take care of her. On that Sunday afternoon when it was time for her to go back, she refused to get in the car. She didn't want to go back to that place. That place where people shuffled aimlessly up and down the hallway, mumbling to themselves. Where they were slumped over in chairs lined up, side by side, against the wall. So, my parents called our family doctor. He drove all the way out from Cambridge to our farm to give Lucy a needle in her arm that reduced her to jelly at the kitchen table. Then, he and my father carried her out to the car, and put her in the back seat. My mom told me and Ava to squeeze in beside her and we drove her back to the hospital. We never talked about it.

I hear a gunshot off in the distance that jolts me back to the groundhog in the woodpile. Tears stream down my red cheeks, turning icy in the frigid air.

The grey clouds part, and shafts of late afternoon sunlight stream down through the trees. I realize that I don't do anything about the groundhog because, somewhere deep down, I know there is nothing I can do for her now.

Her tiny, struggling breath slows down. Then, there is one short, final gasp and it is silent.

I place my bare hand quietly on the logs and turn my tear-stained face up to the sky, inhaling the late afternoon winter air. I feel the groundhog's spirit float away. Shafts of sun dance among the treetops. The wind spirits waft around me, through me. The tree-tops bend and bow in rapture.

My knees are cold and soaked from kneeling in the snow beside the woodpile. I stand up and look back at my fire, now smoldering.

Then, a rush of a thousand tiny groundhogs flows into the rivers inside of me, swirling and swimming through the tunnels in my marrow, laughing and singing through my bones.

2
Science class, 1987

"Hey, Herteis!" I whisper to my grade eleven science partner. I dump my books on the table and sit down beside her, breathless. I made it to class on time.

Lori's notebook is open in front of her. She's wearing white canvas Tretorn tennis shoes, blue Levi's, and a red polo shirt. She looks good in red.

"Hey, Hancock!" She looks up from her notebook and tucks her shoulder-length dirty-blonde hair behind one ear.

"Just seconds before the bell again, eh? Nice one."

Her greenish-grey eyes shine at me from behind thick glasses.

Lori lives on Wrigley Road, two roads over from Alps Road, where I live with my family. Country kids like Lori and me ride the bus to and from school. I hate taking the bus. Cool kids get rides with their parents. The *really* cool kids have their own wheels.

Sometimes, if we're lucky, my mom or dad drives my sisters and me to school in the morning. Usually, we take the bus home after school because they work until five. Lori rides the bus pretty much all the time, unless her coach drops her off at home after practice.

Outside of science class, Lori and I don't hang out together. But there's something about her that I like. She's smart. She seems confident. She's cool, but in a nerdy kind of way. She plays field hockey, softball, and soccer. A couple of times, I've spotted her leaving the change room in her soccer shorts. Her thighs look smooth, solid, and strong in those shorts. She swaggers when she walks, jutting her head slightly out from her neck, like a chicken strutting around a barnyard.

Her boyish voice cracks a little when she talks. She doesn't go on about having sex with boys, getting married, and having kids when she grows up, drinking peach schnapps, doing hash bongs, taking the pill, or feeling hungover, like me and my friends do.

Lori and her friends talk about school assignments, their grades, and sports. They are polite and well-behaved. They hand their assignments in on time, participate in class, joke around with their teachers, and make the honour roll.

Mr Heffernan stands at the front of the room. He is a tall, hunched-over, soft-spoken oaf of a man with wire-rim glasses, disheveled sandy-gray hair, a kind face, and weak classroom management skills. "Good morning, class. Please take your seats. We will get started in a minute. I'm just looking for something—" his voice trails off as he digs around in the breast pocket of his beige corduroy blazer. He shuffles through some papers and fumbles around on his desk.

Students sit in pairs at science tables with Bunsen burner hookups and small sinks with chrome taps. Carolyn, Melissa, Hannah, Bailey, my best friend, and Lori and I sit up near the front. Steve is an arrogant, lanky boy with dark brown hair and a British accent. He sits in the back beside Adam, a tall, skinny, red-haired stoner with heavy-lidded eyes who can barely string two words together. Steve passes a small, folded note up to Hannah.

She opens up the tiny paper package. I look over to see what's in it. There are minuscule hearts scribbled in red pen beside a 7-digit phone number, and a short message that reads "Will you go out with me?" A little pile of pubic hair sits in the crease of the paper. Hannah shrieks as the pubic hair slides off the paper and falls onto her lap. Her face lights up in a mixture of amusement and disgust.

"Oh my god! Gross!" I gag.

Why any girl would be flattered by any of the things Steve does to get their attention is beyond me. I turn away and hide my face on Lori's shoulder. She smells like boy's deodorant.

"Steve is such a pig!" I whisper loudly to Lori.

"Totally. He's an ass," she rolls her eyes.

Mr Heffernan clears his throat.

"Today, with your partners, you will be using your Bunsen burners to conduct experiments with iodine and water. Then, we will be discussing the physical and chemical changes of the substances you will be working with."

He picks up a piece of chalk from the dusty aluminum trough below the chalkboard. He coughs into his hand, leaving a white smudge of chalk on his lips.

"But before we start, let's review. Will someone please tell me one of the safety rules when using a Bunsen burner?" He glances around the room. Carolyn sticks up her hand.

"Yes, Carolyn?"

"Don't put any flammable substances next to your Bunsen burner?"

"Correct," Mr Heffernan writes her answer on the blackboard. The corner of his white button-down hangs down below his corduroy sports jacket.

"Anyone else? Another safety rule?" he asks. His eyes dart around the room.

I look out the window at the row of portables at the edge of the school property, thinking about last weekend. My boyfriend, Ryan, his friends, and I were hanging out at Ryan's parents' house, drinking. Ryan and his friends drank Molson Canadian and I drank Rockaberry Canada Coolers. We all smoked cigarettes. Ryan's friends talked about the girls they had had sex with. They talked about what they did with the girls and made jokes about their bodies. They laughed and punched each other in the shoulders. I just sat there and drank and smoked and laughed once in a while. I hoped Ryan didn't talk like that about me when I wasn't there.

"Hancock, pay attention," Lori elbows me.

I shake my head and look down. Handouts are piled on the desk in front of me. I look over at Lori. She is writing in her notebook. Shit, I just missed the entire review on Bunsen burner safety. I slump back in my chair. I'm behind again.

I take a handout and pass the rest of the pile to the student sitting behind me. Science just isn't that interesting to me. I wish Lori and I could get out of here somehow. I look out the window again. The portables blur.

"Lori and Katie, will you please take the attendance down to the office before we start?" Lori and I nod in agreement. Mr Heffernan hands Lori the attendance sheet. We walk out into the empty hallway.

"Make sure you're back in five minutes," he calls after us.

"Yeah, yeah." I dismiss his words in the air with a flip of my hand.

As Lori and I walk, I run my fingers along the locks on the lockers that line the hallway. The locks clang as they hit the grey metal.

"Hancock! Cut it out. You're going to disturb the classes," Lori admonishes me quietly.

I thrust my hands in my pockets and keep walking. The speckled linoleum of the floor gleams under fluorescent lights above. I try to think of something to say. Lori strides a few steps ahead of me. I smile at her chicken strut walk. Her shoulders are square and her arms swing slightly as she moves. I can see the outline of her triceps dipping below the short sleeves of her polo shirt. I think about how her thighs look in her soccer shorts.

"Fuck, science is so boring," I groan.

I search my mind for something—anything—to talk about rather than school. But, my mind is blank.

Lori turns her head towards me, peering over the rims of her glasses.

"Aw, I don't mind science. You just kind of have to roll with it, Hancock, you know? Just pay attention in class. You'll be fine."

She raises her eyebrows, and smiles. My breath catches in my throat. Why does it feel like she can see right through me?

"Besides, we need a grade eleven science credit to get our diploma," she says.

We pass a couple of grade 12 girls standing at their open lockers, whispering and giggling to each other. Magazine cut-out photos of American actors, Andrew McCarthy, Judd Nelson, and Rob Lowe are taped over the vents on the inside of their locker doors. They stop whispering and look at us as we walk by.

"Uh, I—I—" I hesitate. "I—I don't think we need the credit. Grade ten science is all we need, as far as I know." Why can't I think of something interesting to say?

"Well," Lori shrugs. "I need it I'm going to go into teaching eventually. Hey, I gotta stop at the bathroom, okay?" She waves the attendance sheet in the air as she turns the corner and heads for the girls' bathroom.

"Sure."

I look down the hall and see the principal, Mr Carlton, marching towards us.

"Miss Hancock. Miss Herteis. What are you two up to?" He stops in front of us, looking at me.

"Just using the washroom before taking the attendance to the office, sir," I say.

He looks at Lori and nods.

"Nice game the other day, Lori."

"Thanks, Mr Carlton."

He looks back at me, his voice stern. "Be quick in there and hurry back to class."

Continuing down the hallway, he vanishes around the corner.

Lori opens the door to the girls' bathroom and walks in. I follow. I lean up against the tiled wall beside the sink. Pink industrial liquid soap oozes from the bottom of the soap dispenser and forms a small glistening puddle on the floor below. Cigarette smoke hangs in the air.

"Oh man! One of those head-banger girls was smoking in here again," Lori says as she hands me the attendance sheet. She disappears into one of the pink stalls.

"It was probably Michelle Smith. You know that skinny chick who wears the Iron Maiden t-shirts all the time?" I scoff. "I've seen her smoking in here before."

I hear Lori unbuckle her belt, unzip her jeans, and pull her pants down. Then, the sound of pee hitting water. Below the bathroom stall door, her white tennis shoes poke out from under a pile of denim around her ankles.

I smoked a cigarette at recess. I wonder what Lori would think if she saw me smoking. She's such an athletic girl and I'm not. I mean, I do active stuff outside of school but I'm not one of those team player types. But I don't really consider myself a smoker either. I just do it because my friends do it and it would piss my parents off if they knew.

I reach into my back pocket, and pulling out a piece of watermelon-flavoured Bubblicious, I unwrap it, and pop it into my mouth. Looking in the mirror, I lick my thumbs and run them below my eyes to get rid of smudged eyeliner. I spread grape-flavoured Bonne Bell lip gloss on my lips and pucker my mouth.

Leaning back against the wall, I tug at a lock of my long, dirty-blonde hair, inspecting it for split ends.

The toilet flushes. Lori emerges from the stall and steps over to the sink. After washing and drying her hands, she turns to face me.

"Ready, Hancock?"

The room disappears. All I see is her standing in front of me.

"Not just yet," I say.

I move my body up against hers and give her a peck on the lips. She pulls back, her eyes wide.

"Sorry," I take a step back.

"I guess I've been wanting to do that for a while."

"It's okay. It's, uh, just—I—I've never kissed a girl before."

"Me neither."

"I've never kissed anyone actually," she admits.

"Oh! Okay." I giggle. "Is it okay?"

"Yeah, it's okay," her voice cracks.

"Good, cuz, you just kind of have to roll with it, Herteis," I smirk, feeling bolder.

She throws her head back and laughs. I notice blonde peach fuzz at the crook of her jaw. I laugh, too.

She tips her head down and faces me again. A one-centimeter scar lies diagonally across her chin. A few freckles dance across her face. There's a small, red mark on the bridge of her nose where her glasses sit. With her finger, she shoves her glasses back up the bridge of her nose. She looks at me. Her mouth is directly in front of mine.

I press my lips to hers again. Her mouth is soft and moist. She parts her lips slightly. I part mine. Our tongues touch. Hers tastes sweet and minty, like Trident gum. I'm so glad I had some bubblegum on hand. I let go of the attendance sheet and it floats to the floor. I put my hands on her hips. I can feel her hipbones through her jeans. She hooks her forefingers into the belt loops on my Levi's and pulls my hips against hers. I feel her breasts press against mine.

Is this actually happening?

I open my eyes, slowly. Her face is right there. Her eyes are closed and her head is tilted to the side as she kisses me. I move my hand down to find the seam of her polo shirt. I tug it loose from her jeans and reach underneath, still watching her. My fingers graze her skin. It's smooth and soft. I feel her stomach rising and falling under my palm.

Yep, it's happening.

Me and Lori Herteis. Two girls. In the bathroom at school. During class time. What if someone walks in and sees us? This would spread like wildfire through the school. We would be so screwed. They would kick us out of school for sure.

Behind Lori, I make out the words "A.C. is a dyke" scratched into one of the metal bathroom stall doors.

I think about hearing the words "dyke," "carpet-muncher," and "lesbo" in the hallways at school.

I think about the feeling of darkness that pools in my body when I hear those words, like I want to hide somewhere, like I hope that no-one can see inside me.

I think about the porn that was on the television one night at a party at Adam's house and how the two women and a guy were having a threesome and how the guy was all hairy and eager and I didn't understand why the women wanted him to touch their bodies.

I think about how I tried to pretend I wasn't interested. How I drank my beer and talked and laughed with my friends but I kept stealing glances at the TV screen out of the corner of my eye. How I wished that the guy wasn't in the movie at all and that it was just the two women.

Lori didn't look like the women in that movie. She looked way better. More tough, more androgynous, more real. I close my eyes.

"We've got to stop," she breathes into my ear, but she doesn't move away. Her fingernails scrape my shoulder blade. My lungs feel like they are about to burst out of my ribcage.

I feel a tug on the sleeve of my shirt. The bathroom scene fades and the portables of the school outside come into focus. I hear Lori's voice. "Hey Hancock! Buddy! Are you going to help me out with this experiment or what?" I shake my head and turn away from the window. Lori stares at me, her head tipped to one side.

"Oh shit, sorry," I say, my face growing hot. I feel flustered.

"What do you need me to do?"

"Buddy, pay attention!" She laughs and slaps my shoulder.

"Here, light the Bunsen Burner," she says. "I'll add the iodine to the beaker."

She hands me the lighter. I turn the dial to open the gas line. I click the lighter and hold the flame to the burner.

3
Orange blouse, red lipstick

One day, you and I
are standing in the kitchen of our family farmhouse
and you say
"Why don't you put on
that orange blouse
and some of that red lipstick
and we'll go over to
Jim's for a while?"

I don't remember if we went to Jim's place
which was down the road a few kilometers.

In fact, I don't remember anything after that.
But, in a way, it doesn't matter.

Because those words you spoke to me that day
already told me everything I needed to know
about my worth.

4
Melissa's pub, 1989

Content warning: This story contains details of substance abuse and sexual assault.

I am eighteen years old and it's the summer before my final year of high school—the first summer I get to spend away from home.

Away from my restrictive parents and 11 p.m. curfews and the "no boys in your bedroom" rule.

Away from the hassle of having to hide my addictions from them: tobacco, alcohol, hash, weed, mushrooms, acid.

Away from those sexist high school narratives that girls are sluts if they have sex with boys, but boys are studs if they have sex with girls.

Away from the worry of what others think of me.

I'm staying with my Uncle Hugh. He lives alone in a condo in the town of Canmore, 20 minutes down Highway 1 from Banff. Hugh is my favourite uncle.

When I was young, I wanted to be like him: someone who moved out west, far away from his family in southern Ontario. Who lived with his dog by himself in an alpine town. Who skied powdery mountains in the winter and went fly fishing for rainbow trout during the summer. Who didn't stay stuck in a life that everyone else wanted for him. Who did what he wanted. Who seemed carefree.

Tonight, I'm at a pub called Melissa's in Banff. Banff, a world-class ski town nestled in the Canadian Rockies in Alberta, is known for its transient population of young people, ski bums, climbers, mountaineers, and partiers. Sulphur Mountain lies south across the Bow River from Banff Avenue, the main street, while Mount Rundle's colossal, sloped rump lies to the southeast, beyond Tunnel Mountain.

Loud music pumps overhead as Kenny, Kelly, Steph, and I squeeze in among the crowd of bodies at the bar. Kenny motions to one of the bartenders. With thinning blonde hair and a clean-shaven face, the bartender looks like he is in his early thirties.

"Hi. What can I get you?" he asks Kenny over the din of loud pop music. "Highballs are a buck fifty tonight." He surveys Steph and Kelly. Then, his eyes rest on me for a second.

"Jack and Coke. Thanks, man," Kenny yells.

"Hey! Rye and ginger, thanks," shouts Steph.

Kelly hollers, "I'll have a rum and Coke, please!"

Standing on the brass bar at the bottom of the counter, I lean in towards the bartender and yell, "I'll have a screwdriver, please."

He smirks at me, raising his eyebrows. Using my fingers to tousle my long blonde hair, I smile back at him. Stepping off the brass bar, and pull a tube of my favourite Wet 'n' Wild lipstick out of my pocket and touch up my lips. Red matte. It goes well with my low-cut, short-sleeved blouse and denim mini-skirt.

The bartender fixes our drinks and places them on the bar in front of us, slinging a white hand towel over his shoulder.

Slapping a ten-dollar bill down on the bar for our drinks, Kenny announces, "This round's on me."

He clinks his glass against mine. "Welcome to Banff, Katie."

"Aw, thanks, Kenny! You're the best," I beam.

I met Kenny one day while walking down 8th Street in Canmore with Hugh. Kenny's dad owns the Ford dealership in town, so Kenny has decent wheels—a big, blue Ford F-Series pick-up truck. Kenny is tall and solid, like a grizzly bear. He has kind brown eyes, rosy cheeks, and short brown hair that wisps around his ears. He always wears a ball cap. There's a space between his two front teeth when he smiles. When he laughs, he giggles like a little boy and his whole face lights up.

"Glad you could join us, Katie. We're going to have fun tonight, girl!" Steph declares, pushing a thick strand of long, blonde, spiral-permed hair out of her face. "Melissa's gets packed on Tuesday nights."

"Alright," I yell. This is my first night out to a bar since arriving over a week ago.

"Let's get wasted!" I take a gulp of my screwdriver.

"Yahoo!" Kenny bellows. "We've got ourselves a wild one here."

Kelly and Steph laugh. Kelly and Steph are Kenny's friends—Canmore girls.

The four of us sit down at a small round table in the middle of the floor. People are milling about all around us. Flashing lights pirouette and bounce around the whole room, dancing off of gyrating bodies. Sipping my drink, I feel the weight of my life in southern Ontario, like a drab, heavy, lumpy overcoat, slip away.

Kelly lights up a cigarette and tells Steph and Kenny a story. It's hard to hear what she's saying above the thumping music. But it doesn't matter. I like watching her as she talks. She's pretty. Her long, straight, chestnut-brown hair is swept away from her pink cheeks and fastened with a silver barrette at the back of her head near the top. Her bangs are curled and puffed up with hairspray. Her button nose crinkles when she smiles, and her big brown eyes dance behind long, mascaraed eyelashes. She throws her head back when she laughs. I look away. Girls aren't supposed to look at other girls. But she's cute, and fun and full of life. I want to be like her.

Shaking my head, I drain my glass and think to myself, *Time for another drink*. The waitress comes by our table, and I order the next round. This time, I ask for a double.

When she returns with our drinks, I take a big swig. The vodka stings my nostrils as I exhale. As Kelly, Steph, and Kenny keep talking, I light up a cigarette.

"She Drives Me Crazy" by the Fine Young Cannibals comes on the speaker. Kelly and Steph look at each other and scream.

"I love this song!" Steph screeches.

"Me, too! Let's dance!" Kelly shrieks. She grabs my hand and jumps up. My heart thumps. I lurch to my feet. She and Steph lead me downstairs to the dance floor. Kenny lumbers after us.

We wind our way around the sweaty, jostling bodies to the middle of the dance floor.

Hands in the air, we twirl and sway, wiggle and shake. We throw our heads back and sing as loud as we can:

She drives me crazy! Ooh! Ooh!
Like no-one else! Ooh! Ooh!
She drives me crazy
And I can't help myself!

Kenny shakes his head, laughing, his hands in the front pockets of his jeans. He wobbles around on the dance floor and shuffles his feet. He takes his ball cap off, wipes the sweat off his brow with his forearm, and puts his cap back on.

I grab his arm and lean into his body, standing on my tiptoes.

"Thanks for bringing me here, Ken!" I yell into his ear. I pull back and smile at him, crinkling my nose like Kelly. He grins at me, showing the space between his two front teeth. His cheeks are round and flushed.

"Anytime, Katie! I'm glad you're having fun," he bellows. I flip my long hair back, grab his hand, and pirouette under his out-stretched arm, grinding my hips into his, giggling. Looking up at the ceiling, he shakes his head and laughs. I can see the dimples in his smiling cheeks as multi-coloured lights streak across his face. The bass pounds in my chest and the muscles in my legs feel like Jell-O from the vodka. I am lightheaded.

"She Drives Me Crazy" starts to fade, and Phil Collins' "Two Hearts" swells from the speakers. I grab Kenny's other hand, and we move around each other, whooping and reeling. I step on his foot by mistake and fall into his arms, dissolving into laughter. He swings me around.

Well, there's no easy way to, to understand it
There's so much of my life in her
And it's like I'm blinded
And it teaches you to never let go
There's so much love you'll never know
She can reach you no matter how far, or wherever you are

Kenny drops my hands and yells, "I'll be back."

He turns around and saunters through the damp, frolicking bodies towards the bar. The crowd swallows him up. I twirl around and dance with Steph and Kelly. We shake our heads and clap our hands to the beat, gyrating around each other.

A couple of minutes later, Kenny emerges from the crowd with a tray of four tequila shots with wedges of lemon on top. We each take a shot glass and hold it up in the air together.

"Cheers!" we holler.

Tipping our heads back, Kenny, Steph, Kelly, and I slam the clear liquid in one gulp. For a split second, I feel like I'm going to be sick. Squeezing my eyes shut, I shove the lemon wedge into my mouth and bite down on the sour flesh, sucking the juice out. A warm flush floods my body.

We dance and dance and dance. The lights flash and swirl and flicker through the darkness. Bass throbs through me. Drums pound in my ears. Perspiration drips from my forehead. My hair is damp. People's faces are blurry. The air is moist with sweat. I meet Kenny's eyes. We smile at each other. I sneak glances at Kelly. She sways to the music, her eyes closed. I feel dizzy, giddy.

At the end of the night, I manage to sway towards the bar and hoist myself on a bar stool. People are stumbling out into the cool summer mountain air. I don't know where Kenny, Steph, and Kelly are. The bartender with the thinning blonde hair slides over to me, smiling.

Do you want a drink, beautiful? He asks. "Anything you want," he adds.

"Sure, why not?" I slur. Forming words is difficult. "A seabreeze, please."

"You got it." He grabs a glass tumbler, places it on the bar, adds a small scoop of ice. Fishing a carton of grapefruit juice out of the fridge, he fills the tumbler half full. He pulls a small black hose off its peg below the bar, aims it over the tumbler, and presses one of the buttons on top. Dark pink cranberry juice squirts into the glass. Next, he snatches a bottle of vodka off the shelf, fills up a shot glass, dumps it into the tumbler, and drops a maraschino cherry into the pink drink. He slaps a cocktail napkin down in front of me and sets the tumbler on top.

"Seabreeze. On the house."

"Wow, thanks!" I smile at him. I take a swig and wince.

"That's a lot of vodka," I say, shaking my head and exhaling.

"Anytime." He tosses a little piece of ice down the front of my blouse and winks at me.

He's flirting with me, I think to myself. I grin and look away. I take another slurp of my Seabreeze. The vodka burns going down.

"Like a Prayer" by Madonna radiates the speakers.

When you call my name, it's like a little prayer
I'm down on my knees, I wanna take you there
In the midnight hour, I can feel your power
Just like a prayer, you know I'll take you there

As I sit at the bar, a few people filter slowly out the door and into the warm summer air. Two women with long blonde hair in short miniskirts have their arms around each other's shoulders as they stagger outside, whooping and hollering. Their boyfriends shuffle out behind them.

The bartender grabs a couple of cubes of ice from underneath the bar and walks over to me. He looks at me and tosses the ice into the opening of my blouse again. The ice is cold as it slides down my skin. I toss my head back and laugh.

"So, sexy, wanna come home with me?" he asks, raising his eyebrows, smirking. "I live just a few blocks away. I can drive you home in the morning on my motorcycle."

Am I going to get lucky tonight?, I think.

"Sure, why not?" I shrug, smiling. "I'll have to tell my friends."

"Great," he says.

He tosses the other ice cube into his mouth, chews it slowly, staring intently at me. There's a strange, fleeting feeling in my stomach that I can't place. I take another gulp of my Seabreeze.

"I'm almost done here." He turns and walks to the other end of the bar to serve a customer.

Swivelling around on my barstool, I see Kenny, Kelly, and Steph walking off the dance floor, laughing. They smile as they saunter towards me. Sweaty, intoxicated people continue to disperse, tilting and reeling towards the door of the pub.

"Hey Katie! There you are," Kenny shouts over the music. "I was looking for you. We're ready to go."

"Thanks, guys. But I think I'm going to stay in town for the night. I have a date," I smirk, nodding my head in the direction of the bartender.

Kenny's mouth drops open, like he's been slapped in the face. He surveys the bartender. With wide eyes, Kelly and Steph fish cigarettes and lighters out of their purses.

"Okay! Well, see you around, Katie. Have fun!" Steph howls as she whirls out the door.

Kelly stops, a cigarette dangling from between her lips.

"Are you sure?" she asks, putting her hand on my arm.

"Yeah, I'm good, Kelly. Thanks." I wave my hand, dismissing her.

Shrugging, she turns on her heel, and teeters outside to the parking lot.

Kenny turns to me. "No, Katie. You should come with us." His tone is serious.

"You don't even know him." His eyebrows knit together in a frown.

"Aw, Kenny, you're sweet," I drawl.

"It's okay! I'm fine. He's nice!"

"Pffft! Yeah. Nice?" Kenny scoffs, loudly. "How are you going to get back to Canmore?" He eyes me, eyebrows raised.

"He said he would give me a ride."

Taking another sip of my drink, I swing my bare legs back and forth on my barstool.

"Katie, you're really drunk," Kenny pleads. I get that strange feeling in my stomach again.

"Kenny, I really am. And, you're being so serious!"

Brushing off the expression on his face—a mixture of worry and sadness—I poke his broad chest, throw my head back, and giggle.

"It's okay. Don't worry! I'll be fine!" I take a sip of my drink and smile at him, ignoring the tremor in my stomach.

Kenny looks away. He shakes his head. He looks back at me briefly before spinning around and striding out the door. I watch him vanish into the night. I finish the rest of my drink and put the empty glass on the bar. The bartender strides over to me.

"Okay, I can leave now. Let's go," he motions to me.

He turns back to the bar and hollers to one of the other bartenders.

"Thanks for covering for me, Mike!"

"No problem, Tim. You owe me!" Mike shouts.

He beams at me and looks back at Tim, giving him a "thumbs-up."

"Have fun, buddy!"

I blush. Tim walks ahead of me out the door. I follow him. The night air feels fresh on my face. It's mixed with the scent of pine trees and cigarette smoke.

"So, what's your name anyway?" he asks, as he puts his arm around my shoulders.

"Katie."

"Well, it's nice to meet you, Katie."

"You're Tim," I slur. I can feel the vodka coursing through my veins, numbing my muscles, muffling the night sounds around me. I like this feeling, the feeling of not feeling my body. I feel warm. Hazy. Pliable.

"Tim, the cute bartender at Melissa's Pub."

I giggle, feeling pleased with myself. I'm far away from my life in Ontario. I'm going to have a one-night stand with a guy I don't know. No one knows me here. No one will judge me.

I lean my shoulder into Tim's as we walk. I feel woozy. My knees buckle slightly and I lose my balance. Laughing, I grab for his torso.

"Hey, hey, okay," Tim chuckles, holding me up. "I've got you. Let's get you back to my place. It's just around the corner."

When we arrive at his apartment building, Tim takes me downstairs to the basement where the sauna is. He opens the big wooden door. The sweet smell of hot cedar wood spills out and fills my nostrils. We step inside, strip down to our underwear, and sit on the warm bench.

He drapes one arm around my waist. It feels heavy. He puts his other hand on the back of my neck and tugs me toward him. He kisses me. I kiss him back. His arm around my waist tightens.

He nibbles my neck, hard and clumsy. The strange feeling in my stomach returns. It's stronger this time, hammering inside me. Telling me something.

"Ow, Tim! That hurts," I giggle nervously. I push him away.

"Slow down." I wriggle my body, trying to loosen his embrace.

He pulls back and sneers at me with blazing eyes.

"No way. You're gorgeous," he growls and tightens his grip. Cold surges through me. His fingers pinch the skin on my thighs.

"Ouch, Tim! That really does hurt." I squeal, trying not to sound scared.

He nibbles on my shoulders with his teeth and then, nips the flesh on my breasts.

"Ouch, Tim, please."

My heart is thumping. The hammering in my stomach is relentless.

I know I'm in trouble. Thoughts flood my brain.

I have to get out of here. If I get away, where will I go? It's the middle of the night.

How will I get back to Canmore by myself? Could I hail a cab at the gas station?

What will I tell Hugh? Kenny? Why didn't I just go back to Canmore with Kenny?

What if I tell Tim I want to go home and he turns violent?

Fear surges through my body. Then, I can't feel anything.

Don't piss him off. Just go along with it. It will be over soon and then you can get out of here.

Tim stands up and grabs my hand.

"C'mon, Katie. Let's go upstairs."

Like a good girl, I get to my feet. As I follow him upstairs, my limbs feel like cement. I hold the banister on the way up and look behind me to make sure I remember the way out. I feel like I'm walking the plank of a pirate ship with my hands tied behind my back. Like I'm steps away from falling down into a deep, dark, cold ocean.

In his apartment, we lie on his bed and start fooling around. Yanking off my underwear, he rams his penis inside me.

Pound. Pound. Pound. Pound. Pound. Pound. Pound. Pound. Pound. Pound.

It goes on and on.

And on.

And on.

And on.

Finally, I tell Tim that I've had enough. He ignores me. I tell him again. He pumps and grinds and mashes his hips into mine.

Pound. Pound. Pound. Pound. Pound. Pound. Pound. Pound. Pound. Pound.

"Please stop. Get off me," I beg. "Please."

Pound. Pound. Pound. Pound. Pound. Pound. Pound. Pound. Pound. Pound.

Shoving my hands up against his chest, I try and push him off me.

Pound. Pound. Pound. Pound. Pound. Pound. Pound. Pound. Pound. Pound.

With the weight of him on top of me, it's hard to breathe. I can't feel my body, but I know it's sliding up and down the sheets.

Crying, I pummel his chest with my fists.

Pound. Pound. Pound. Pound. Pound. Pound. Pound. Pound. Pound. Pound.

I turn my head towards the window beside the bed. Tears run down the bridge of my nose and my temple, soaking the lumpy pillow.

Pound. Pound. Pound. Pound. Pound. Pound. Pound. Pound. Pound. Pound.

I think about Kenny and Kelly and Steph.

I think about having fun with them, drinking and dancing at Melissa's. I think about Kelly's pretty smile and her crinkly nose when she laughs.

I think about Kenny trying to convince me to come back to Canmore with them.

I peer through the window into the night. Searching for the colossal form of Mt. Rundle, I plead silently that she will turn into a gigantic superhero made of Paleozic sedimenatary rock and appear outside Tim's apartment. That, with her boulder-sized hands, she will rip off the wall of his bedroom and come thundering in, raging like she's been asleep for millions of years and is ready to cause some feminist shit. That she will pull Tim off me and grind him into a pile of mucky flesh, and broken bones, and smeared blood under her massive, stoney fists. That she will yank me off the bed, and cradle me in her mammoth craggy arms, as she storms away from the apartment. That she will throw me up on her wide rocky shoulders and we will rumble down Highway 1 together, heading back to Canmore. To Hugh's place. To my bed there. To safety.

But nothing happens. It's pitch-black outside and I can't see anything out the window. Mt. Rundle isn't coming to save me.

No one is coming to save me while this man does what he wants to me. Rapes my body.

My body. My sweet, naïve, eighteen-year-old body.

The body that has carried me through this life so far.

That walks through alfalfa fields and forests of maple on our farm in southern Ontario.

That embraces our beloved pets: two dogs, numerous goats, a potbelly pig, a cat.

That lays down in fields of long, yellow summer grasses, gazing up at the blue sky.

That is filled up with music and plays guitar and loves to sing.

The body I have known and tried to love my whole life.

The body that feels deeply.

The body that tried to warn me.

The body that I betrayed.

My heart is splitting into pieces. *This is what I get for being so easy. For going home with some guy I don't know. Maybe if I fall asleep, this will be over once I wake up.*

I stop resisting. Tim is still on top of me as I close my eyes. A grey fog saturates my mind. Then, everything goes dark.

I wake up later in the night. He is still on top of me.

Pound. Pound. Pound.

I close my eyes again, letting the darkness wash over me.

****

The next morning, I open my eyes. The sun is shining outside, Mt. Rundle is bathed in light.

Tim is snoring beside me. He is drooling on the pillow. There is a stinging ache between my legs. What happened last night creeps into my mind.

"Hey, Tim. Wake up." I shake his shoulder.

"I have to work today."

He groans and rolls over. He opens his eyes and looks at me. His eyes are hollow. Whatever attracted me to him last night at Melissa's Pub is gone.

"Yeah," he moans, rubbing his eyes. "I'm getting up."

Wordlessly, we roll off his bed and pull on our clothes. Suddenly, I gag. Stumbling to the bathroom, I pitch forward over the toilet and throw up. I have a searing headache, but I decide to not ask for any aspirin or coffee. I just want to get out of there and go back to Canmore. At the sink, I rinse my mouth with the hottest water I can stand and exit the bathroom.

As we leave, Tim closes and locks the apartment door behind us. We walk down the stairs, push the door open, and go outside into the wide-open air.

The sweet, pungent fragrance of pine trees soothes me. I open my mouth and fill my lungs with the biggest breath I can manage to pull in. A couple of crows are discussing the day's pursuits in a treetop down the street. A grey jay swoops down from a rooftop to inspect us, searching for a possible handout: a morsel of muffin or croissant. No such luck today.

Tim trudges to the curb where his motorcycle is parked. I follow. He shoves a key into the ignition of his motorbike and it roars to life. He hops on, puts on his helmet, and hands me the extra one that's attached to the back of the bike. Jamming it on my head, I do up the strap under my chin and get on the back of the bike. Looking for handles to hold on to beside my seat, I see none. I will myself to wrap my arms around his waist. I feel like I'm going to be sick again. I take a deep breath and pull my abdominal muscles back as hard as I can so that my torso doesn't touch his back. He pulls away from the curb and heads towards Highway 1, east. To Canmore.

When we arrive at the edge of town, I ask Tim to drop me off on the corner of Railway Avenue and 8th Street by the Drake Inn, five blocks from Hugh's condo. I don't want Tim to know where I'm living for the summer.

He maneuvers his bike up against the curb. I slip off the bike, remove the helmet, and hand it back to him, smiling weakly.

"See ya around," he says.

"Yeah. See ya," I reply.

He revs up his engine and speeds off.

I turn and start walking north up 8th Street. I never see Tim again.

5
High

In the living room of my top-floor apartment at 1606 Nanaimo Street, I plop down onto the threadbare, tan-coloured sofa chair I bought from Value Village for twenty bucks, throwing my bare legs over the arm. Across from where I sit, there's a worn, beige loveseat I dragged in from the back alley and beside that, an overturned red milk crate that doubles as a side table. Reaching over to the scuffed oak wood coffee table, I snatch up *The Tao of Pooh* by Benjamin Hoff. I turn to the page with the folded down corner. I heard about this book from Damian, so I bought a second-hand copy at a used bookstore on Commercial Drive.

In *The Tao of Pooh*, I learn about the basic principles of Taoism through the gentle, uncomplicated, sometimes insightful, soft-voiced, fictional British teddy bear, Winnie the Pooh, brought to life in A. A. Milne's books for children. *The Tao of Pooh* is for adults—though, young adults like me who want to practice letting go of anxiety and finding joy in simple living. After all, I just moved to the beautiful city of Vancouver, British Columbia, on the Pacific west coast of Canada. At 23 years old, with my undergraduate degree completed, I'm starting a new life, almost four thousand kilometres away from where I grew up. It's my life now, and I can do whatever I want.

Pooh's Cottleston Pie Principle provides some clues to guide me:

1.   *Allow things to be what they are.*
2.   *Everyone has limitations.*
3.   *Some things cannot be known.*

Down below, the front door to my apartment opens and the sound of footsteps coming up the creaky wooden stairs gets closer and closer. Damian appears in the doorway to the living room and smiles at me. He's staying the night.

"Hey, babe," he smiles, slipping out of his rubber Merrill sandals.

"Hey!" I say, rising off the sofa chair to give him a kiss.

Damian is gorgeous. Confidence radiates off him like electricity. He's 5 ft. 9, 22 years old, and walks with straight, square shoulders. He has a cloud of dark curly, brown hair, full lips, a constellation of small dark moles on one cheekbone, and a dark brown beard. His large brown eyes are framed with long brown eyelashes but are often hidden by dark sunglasses.

Back from the 7-11 corner store, he empties the contents of a plastic bag onto the coffee table: *The Georgia Straight*—Vancouver's entertainment newspaper—a large bottle of guava juice, a bag of Doritos, a fresh pouch of Drum tobacco, and Zig-Zag rolling papers. Sitting down on the loveseat, he reaches to the stack of CDs on top of the milkcrate side table, tugging out the soundtrack from the film *The Harder They Come*. Dropping the CD into the CD player, he presses "play." Horns bleat. Synthesizer chords pulse. Drums beat out a reggae rhythm.

Backed by female harmonies, Jimmy Cliff's smooth voice rings out as he sings:

> *You can get it if you really want*
> *You can get it if you really want*
> *You can get it if you really want*
> *But, you must try, try and try, try and try*
> *You'll succeed at last.*

I wonder why Jimmy Cliff's lyrics seem at odds with the Cottleston Pie Principle. How come Pooh teaches us that we must allow things to be what they are, but Jimmy says if we want something, we must try, try, and try? Some things cannot be known, I guess.

Damian doesn't like the music I listen to—Tracy Chapman, Ani DiFranco, Indigo Girls, Joni Mitchell, Janis Joplin, Tori Amos, Sarah McLaughlin—too feminine, perhaps. But, he would never say that. I also like The Grateful Dead, Bob Dylan, Bruce Cockburn. But, they are too hippie for him. He's upfront about that. It's okay. I'm soaking up everything my new life on the west coast has to offer. I listen to reggae now because it's one of Damian's favourite genres of music. He knows a lot about music.

Damian reads the newspaper. I read my book. We smoke Drum. Ten minutes later, there is a knock on the front door.

"Come in!" Damian yells. He puts down the paper and stands up.

Footsteps thump up the stairs to the living room. In the door-way of our living room appears a tall, trim, pale, bald man. Simon has bright blue eyes and a wide smile with a dimple beside his mouth. A pair of black sunglasses rests on the top of his bare head. Later that summer, when the film *Natural Born Killers* comes out, I tell Damian that Simon looks like Woody Harrelson.

"Hey, brother!" Simon chuckles and reaches out for Damian. They shake hands and hug.

Simon turns to me and smiles. I stand up and step towards him, smiling.

"This must be Katie! So nice to meet Damian's girl," Simon beams. He walks over to me, takes my right hand in both of his and shakes it.

"Hi, Simon. Nice to meet you," I say, shaking his hand.

Damian sits down on the sofa chair and Simon offers me the loveseat.

"Go ahead," I decline. I take a cushion off the loveseat and place it on the hardwood floor. I sit down, Simon sits down and Damian snatches his Zig-Zags and the Drum off the coffee table.

"Nah, nah! Here, buddy!" Simon waves at Damian to put down the Drum. Digging into the pocket on his shirt, he pulls out a pack of du Maurier Lights.

"TMs. Alright!" Damian shrugs and puts the pouch of tobacco and rolling papers back on the coffee table. "TMs" are "tailor-made" cigarettes, not hand-rolled cigarettes, like the ones Damian and I smoke. Drum is cheaper than tailor-made cigarettes. You get a lot more tobacco for your money, but you have to roll it yourself. I used to smoke tailor-mades before I moved to Vancouver. Now, I smoke Drum, like Damian.

Simon fishes out three cigarettes. He puts all three in his mouth, lights them, hands one to Damian, one to me, and keeps one for himself. I move the ashtray to the middle of the coffee table. We draw on our cigarettes at the same time and blow smoke out towards the yellowish-coloured ceiling.

Damian and Simon start complaining about work. Damian works under the table as a roofer and Simon is in construction.

"Christ, my foreman is an asshole." A gust of smoke blasts out of Simon's nostrils.

"Fucking guy is making me work overtime on the long weekend. We got a contract we have to finish by June," he grumbles. "I'm so tired." He sags sideways on the loveseat, the knuckles of his right hand hitting the floor with a thud.

"Shit, man," Damian replies. "I wish I could work overtime. I need the extra cash. But I work for a cheap bastard." Cigarette smoke seeps out from between his lips as he talks.

"But, how about them Leafs, eh buddy?" Damian cuffs Simon in the knee. "They're doing alright."

Simon shoots straight up from the loveseat, like someone just shot his veins full of adrenaline. The Toronto Maple Leafs are Simon's favourite hockey team.

"Oh yeah! I'm praying. I don't believe in God, but I'm praying," he exclaims, smirking as he folds his hands together, his cigarette squeezed between the first two fingers of his left hand. "Too bad about the Habs, though, buddy. Rough."

The Montreal Canadiens—"the Habs"—Damian's favourite team, are based in Montreal, Quebec. "Habs" is colloquial for "habitants," a French word meaning "people who live in a particular place."

The early settlers in Quebec who immigrated from France were called "habitants." The Habs and the Leafs made the playoffs, but the Habs were just eliminated. The Leafs are still in the running.

"Nah, it's all good buddy. The Habs won last year." Damian flicks his right hand dismissively in the air. Cigarette ash falls to the floor.

"They've taken the cup home 24 times. Twenty-four times!" he boasts. "The Leafs, on the other hand, my friend, are a national embarrassment. Maybe this is the year they get their shit together?" He shakes his head, grinning at Simon.

Simon drops his bald head into his hands and slaps it a few times.

"Fuck, don't remind me!" he groans. "They haven't won the Cup since '67! Christ, I wasn't even born yet."

"They better make it all the way this year or I give up," he whines, throwing his hands up in the air.

"Hey Simon, can I get you something? A drink?" I pipe up.

Simon stops talking and turns to me, startled, like he forgot I was there.

"Oh! Nah, thanks, Katie. I'm good." He pauses, drumming his fingertips on the coffee table. "Do you cheer for the Habs, like your old man here does?"

"No." I shrug. "Hockey isn't really my thing."

"Oh, hmm," he replies. "Maybe you should jump on the Leafs bandwagon?" His eyes twinkle.

"Maybe," I smile. There's something endearing about Simon.

He turns back to Damian. They debate about who is going to win the Stanley Cup this year. They talk about hockey stats and who's been traded. I listen. I don't know anything about hockey.

Then, Damian asks about Maureen. Maureen is Simon's room-mate and a friend of Damian's. Simon's shoulders slump and he turns sombre, shifting in his seat.

"Aw, she's alright, man." He shrugs, his eyes darting around the room. A twitch tugs at the corner of his mouth.

"Kind of struggling right now, you know? She's trying to straighten up and get off the base, right? She looks a bit rough. All skinny and shit. Sores on her face. But, you know Mo. She's a tough bitch. She'll get through it." He lights another cigarette and takes a long drag.

"Oh shit! I almost forgot!" Simon hoots. He lurches forward, lays his cigarette in the ashtray, reaches into the back pocket of his jeans, and pulls out his wallet. He opens it and fishes out a tiny, folded package of tin foil. He hands it to Damian.

Damian takes a twenty-dollar bill out of his pocket and gives it to Simon.

"Thanks, brother. Appreciate it." Simon waves the twenty in the air, sticks it in his wallet, and shoves his wallet back into his jeans pocket.

Turning serious for a moment, Simon warns, "You know to take it easy on this stuff, eh? Some of the stuff around town has been potent lately. Mixed with a bit of angel dust. Rat poison. But, don't worry," Simon assures us. "This shit's good."

He reaches over and claps his hand on Damian's shoulder.

"I care about you, brother. I don't want you and your girl here to get messed up," his eyes flash widely at me.

"Yeah, no worries, buddy," Damian smiles. He stands up. "It's all good. Thanks."

Simon jumps up and shakes Damian's hand. They lean in for a hug, and snicker. Simon turns to me, and giving me a salute, kicks the heels of his running shoes together.

"Nice to meet you, Katie," he grins broadly. "See ya 'round!"

Then, he spins around and bounds down the stairs.

"Have fun! Call me anytime!" he yells back at us. The apartment door shuts behind him.

Except for the song, *The Harder They Come*, emanating from the CD player, the room is quiet.

Damian gets up, walks into the kitchen, and pours two glasses of water. Then he disappears down the hall into the bathroom. He returns with the glasses of water and sets them on the living room coffee table. Sitting down in the chair, he moves the coffee table closer to him. I slide my cushion across the floor to sit oppo-site from him, and crossing my legs, I watch.

Damian digs into the pocket of his shorts and lays a ten-dollar bill, a bank card, and a small mirror on the coffee table. He unfolds the little tin foil paper to reveal the fine, cream-coloured powder inside. He gently dumps the powder from the tin foil onto the mirror.

With his bank card, he slides some of the powder away from the pile and creates a smaller pile. Then, he separates the smaller pile into two even smaller piles. Every few seconds, he taps his bank card on the mirror to unstick minute grains of the powder from the card. He sculpts the two small piles of powder into two neat, short lines about centimetre long and a millimetre wide. Rails, he calls them.

I take a drink of water. Sitting in front of a modest pile of heroin with my boyfriend in East Vancouver, far away from my family and my life in Ontario, feels exciting. Bad-ass. I think about when I used to drink, smoke pot and hash, take mushrooms, and drop acid back in Ontario. Booze and drugs removed me from the awareness of my body. Numbed me. Disconnected me from the omnipresent sense my body didn't belong to me but rather, to all the men I dated—and even the ones I didn't. Made me oblivious to the small voice that punctured my mind now and then, asking me if I actually liked men. Allowed me to dissociate when I had sex with them.

Damian puts down the bank card and wipes his hands on his shorts. He looks at me.

"Smack is really strong, Katie. That's why the lines are much smaller than coke," he explains. "It doesn't take much to get high."

"Okay." I nod.

He picks up the ten-dollar bill and rolls it into a tight cylinder.

"We can only do a little at a time. Or, we could overdose." Elbows on his thighs, Damian leans over the mirror on the coffee table.

"Johnny Too Bad" by The Slickers comes on.

Walking down the road with your pistol in your waist
Johnny, you're too bad

Walking down the road with your ratchet in your waist
Johnny, you're too bad…

With the first two fingers of his right hand, Damian sticks the rolled-up bill into his right nostril and plugs his left nostril with the forefinger of his left hand. With his face two inches from the mirror, he places the bill in front of one of the tiny rails. He sniffs evenly, steadily, forcefully, and the powder vanishes up the bill as he pushes it along the mirror.

He sits up and wipes his nose with his left hand. There's a trace of cream-coloured dust between his upper lip and his nose. I reach over and wipe it off with my thumb, smiling. He takes my hand. He winces, shudders, and sniffs hard.

"Argh! It burns a bit," he tells me, pinching the bridge of his nose. Letting go of my hand, he moves the mirror closer towards me. He passes me the rolled-up bill.

"Make sure you inhale hard," he instructs me, sniffing again. "And don't breathe out or you'll blow it everywhere."

I take the rolled-up bill, stick it up my nostril, and crouch over the mirror. I watch the second rail disappear as I sniff. I put the bill down. My eyes water. My sinuses feel like they're on fire. My nose runs. I jerk my head back and sniff. An acrid tang floods my taste buds.

"Shit, it does burn! It's dripping down the back of my throat," I exclaim. I guzzle some water from the glass on the coffee table. "Ugh! It's so bitter."

"Yeah," Damian says. He leans back in the sofa chair, his tanned arms laying on the armrests. He closes his eyes. "I'm rushing," he says.

I climb up onto the loveseat. The evening East Vancouver sunlight streams in through our open living room window. The warm scent of summer wafts in—lilac blossoms, salt air, exhaust fumes, a hint of rotting garbage from the back alley. A black string of crows flies past overhead, heading east, cawing. Seagulls shriek from the rooftop next door. Cars, trucks, and buses roar past down below on Nanaimo Street.

A minute later, a surge of warmth spreads through me.

"Oh," I say. "I think I'm rushing, too. Whoa."

I tip my head back and close my eyes. A hazy heat undulates from my brain throughout my body, swells in my torso, and gushes out to the tips of my fingers and toes. Every nerve in my body pulsates softly. I feel like I'm levitating into the air.

Silently, I melt into the loveseat.

Then, I break out into a sweat.

"I'm going to be sick," I announce, pitching forward off the couch. Staggering through the kitchen, my hand over my mouth, I turn toward the bathroom.

I hear Damian's bellowing laugh behind me.

"That's normal, babe!" he hollers. "It'll pass."

I make it to the bathroom just in time to drop to my knees in front of the toilet. My body heaves. I vomit violently into the white bowl. Another wave of warm euphoria washes through me.

Throwing up isn't so bad when I'm high on heroin, I think to myself. *Not like when I'm hungover from a night of partying.* I throw up again and again.

Then, my stomach softens. My shoulders relax. I stand up and flush the toilet. I wash my hands, brush my teeth, and look in the mirror. My eyes look eerie. My irises, steel blue, are enlarged, and my pupils are minuscule black pinpricks. I tuck a few wayward strands of hair behind my ears and reposition the messy dirty blonde bun at the back of my head. I open the medicine cabinet and apply another layer of alum stone to my moist armpits and swipe some cherry ChapStick across my lips.

I drift back into the living room and slide onto the loveseat.

Damian snorts another rail and hands me the rolled-up bill.

"Once you're sick, you should be good to keep going."

I pull the table closer to me. I snort another tiny rail. The sting in my sinuses reminds me of swimming in a pool when I was a kid and inhaling chlorine pool water through my nose by mistake. I sit up, pinch my nostrils together, and sniff. I gulp some more water to wash the bitter taste down.

A rush radiates through me again. The edges of reality blur into a gentle, fuzzy fog. A soft feeling of bliss envelops me. My body, weightless, is wrapped in a cottony cloud.

Damian pulls out another CD from the pile on the red milk-crate: *Naturally* by J.J. Cale. He joins me on the couch and pulls me close to him.

> *They call me the breeze*
> *I keep blowing down the road*
> *They call me the breeze*
> *I keep blowing down the road*

I lay my head on Damian's shoulder and nuzzle my face in his warm neck. It smells like Dr Bronner's eucalyptus castile soap. I feel protected with his arm wrapped around me. Time slows to a crawl. We nod off.

We come to. I feel like I'm floating. We smoke Drum, drink guava juice, snort more lines, fuck on the loveseat, swap stories about the drugs we've done, and laugh. Around 3 a.m., we slither, naked, onto the futon mattress on the floor in my bedroom and slip into darkness.

The next morning, my eyes flutter open. My temples throb with shooting pain and all of the pores of my body are moist with sweat. I roll off the futon mattress and crawl to the bathroom. I retch over and over into the toilet until all I can do is dry heave. Crumpled on the bathroom floor, I don't have the strength to stand up and walk back to bed. In all my nights of drinking and getting high, I've never been hungover like this. Shaking with agony, I spend the entire day in bed, with a large bowl beside me on the floor in case I can't make it to the bathroom.

Damian and I do heroin again the next weekend. When heroin is coursing through my bloodstream, the uncertainties I have about my life evaporate. I don't worry about who I am or who I will become. I don't fret about how I look, feel, or act, or what I say and what other people say to me and about me. I don't agonize about how I will earn a living in this new city. I don't wonder if I'm ever going to be gutsy enough to leave Damian and date a woman. I don't fixate on what I'm going to do tomorrow, next week, next year, or for the rest of my life. It all dissolves. Heroin gives me permission to allow things to be as they are. Heroin forces me to relax, reminding me that some things cannot be known.

Damian quits his job as a roofer. It's too hard on his body, he tells me. He goes on welfare like me. We'll get jobs in September, we say. We spend the summer hanging out on Commercial Drive, drinking coffee, smoking, reading, and playing backgammon—Damian teaches me how. We go to Hi-Life Records and look at CDs and used vinyl.

Some days—later in the afternoon, because Damian is not a morning person—we drive out to Wreck Beach. Sitting on a brightly-coloured batik blanket on the sand, we lean up against giant driftwood logs. We face the Pacific Ocean and Bowen Island across the water, reading, smoking, and drinking mango juice. Sunlight sparkles on the water and the waves retreat as the tide rolls out and the beach expands. Sand sticks between our toes and fingers and we kiss each other's salty lips. The wind tickles our tanned, sweaty skin as we frolic in the cool sea water.

When we can afford it, we go to a trendy restaurant called WaaZuBee on Commerical Drive. The front of the restaurant has large windows that open onto the street. Inside, the walls are painted black and the lights are turned down really low. Through the dim light, candles burn in tall glass holders with images of Jesus and Mother Mary painted on them. We order French fries with garlic aioli and drink coffee and Damian jokes around with the staff.

My guitar collects dust in the corner of my living room apartment. I haven't played much since I got to Vancouver. I thought about trying my hand at writing a song—my first song—but I'm too busy spending time with Damian. I pawn my Joni Mitchell and Bob Dylan CDs and give up my tickets to go see the Grateful Dead in Eugene, Oregon with a bunch of other friends so I can stay home with Damian and get high. *I'm over the Grateful Dead anyway*, I tell myself. *And besides, I'm in love.*

One night, with a few friends, Damian and I go to a rave downtown hosted by the owner of WaaZuBee. All of the WaaZuBee staff are there and the room is packed with bodies. We take ecstasy for the first time. The booming rhythmic beats of hardcore techno, acid house, and dance music throb in my ears and thump in my chest. The dark, humid room vibrates and everyone looks exquisite. A vibrating mass of damp, gyrating bodies, we sweat, smoke, grind our teeth, smile nonstop, and drink copious amounts of water, basking in the buzz saturating the room.

Around 4 a.m., people meander outside from the party. Our friends left a couple of hours ago. Damian and I decide to leave and walk for a while because we need the fresh air.

"I'll hail us a cab in a bit," Damian says.

It's warm for late summer. The sky is still a dark black-purple, but in the east, a pale blue glow hovers above the horizon. A couple of cars race by. I traipse along the Granville Street Bridge, a few feet behind Damian. Ninety feet underneath us are the salty, deep waters of False Creek.

As I stop to peer over the edge into the darkness below, a dense, viscous dread saturates my flesh. A voice in my brain commands, "Jump, Katie. Jump." Terror courses through me, like an electric current. I grab the handrail, knuckles white with fear. My lungs feel as though they're being squeezed and something is wrapping a dark, heavy cape around my body. The voice whispers again. "Jump, Katie." Death is swirling around me, trying to swallow me up.

"Don't do it," I hiss out loud to myself. "Don't do it."

"Damian!" I yell, my fingers like a vise grip on the handrail. "Damian! I gotta get off this bridge. Now!"

Damian turns around and strides back to me. He puts his hands on my shoulders.

"What's the matter, Katie? Look at me," he demands, shaking me. "Look at me!"

"I-I-I don't know." I shiver. I look at him and then I look away. "I felt like I was going to jump. I gotta get off this bridge. Please."

"Okay, okay. I've got you." He puts his arm around me as a truck thunders by, shaking loose the murky hallucination that gripped me.

"Let's go. You're okay. Just walk with me. I'll hail a cab."

****

At the end of the summer, Damian moves in with me. He gets a full-time job as a high-rise window washer in the business district downtown. He gets Simon a job too and they work together. I get hired by the Vancouver School Board as a full-time Special Education Assistant in a grade four class in a school a few blocks from where we live.

Damian and I do begin doing heroin one night of every weekend. We agree that if we only do it one night a week, we're not addicts.

Months and months roll by. Every now and then, our heroin use spills over onto a weeknight.

A year goes by until one late spring Thursday morning, my alarm goes off at 6:45 a.m. I am still high.

I slip out of bed and get ready for work in a daze.

As I ride my bike down Lakewood Drive towards the school, I realize I'm losing control of my life. How can I work in an elementary school with little kids and have a heroin problem?

Once I arrive at the school, I hurry to a single-stall bathroom near the office, stick my finger down my throat, and make myself throw up in the toilet. I fish my toothbrush and toothpaste out of my knapsack and brush my teeth again. Popping an extra-strength Advil will help keep the headache at bay. I sign in at the office. Thankfully, the student I work with needs to take breaks from the classroom and likes to go outside a lot. Several times that day, he and I go outside to walk around the schoolyard.

After school, I ride my bike a few blocks to Trout Lake and sit by myself on a wooden dock among the bulrushes. As I look out at the water, my head is throbbing. Dread washes over me like a tidal wave.

I am trapped. I have a drug addiction, and a boyfriend with a drug addiction and friends with drug addictions. Working as a Special Education Assistant in a public school doesn't inspire me. Even though I've been living in Vancouver—a city flanked by mountains—for a year now, I haven't gone backcountry hiking or camping at all—something I have long dreamed of doing since I was a child. I don't know what I want to do with my life and I cannot envision my future. I remind myself that some things cannot be known. But, I know I don't want to keep going the way I am. Tears brim behind my eyelids and roll down my face.

I sit on the dock for a while, until I begin to feel cold. Hopping back on my bike, I ride the few blocks home.

I tell Damian that I'm quitting drugs. He says he is going to stop too. I feel relieved. It will be easier if we're on the wagon together, he says. I agree. We hug.

A couple of months later, our relationship is over. He wants to stay in Vancouver, but I want to move out of the city for good, to get away from the party scene we are still immersed in, to start a new life and live in the mountains. I heard about the Kootenays, a mountainous region in the southern interior of British Columbia, from my sister's boyfriend. I want to move there.

Damian and I pack up our things separately. We clean the apartment: sweeping the floors, wiping down the walls and kitchen counter, and disinfecting the bathroom. Carrying the loveseat and the sofa chair outside, we leave them in the back alley. Someone else might be able to use them again. Damian helps me stack my stuff, including the red milk crate jammed with CDs, into the bright yellow GMC camper van parked on the side street that he and I bought for 400 dollars from an ad in the newspaper a few months ago. On the sidewalk, we hug one last time.

With a laundry bag full of clothes, and a large backpack hanging off his shoulders, Damian lights a cigarette, turns away, and saunters west on Graveley Street towards Commercial Drive, his broad shoulders square, smoke drifting up past his dark brown curls.

I go back into the house and plod up the creaky wooden stairs. The June sun shines into the living room window. I look around the quiet, empty apartment, an ache in my heart. *What happened to us? To me? We had so much fun in the beginning. We were so in love. What am I going to do now?* Tears sting my eyelids. *Everyone has limitations.*

Doing one last check of the apartment, I walk back down the stairs for the last time. Pulling the door shut behind me, I lock it and put the key in the mailbox for the landlord. I step over to the van and slide in, jamming the key in the ignition. I start the engine and pull away from the curb, heading east out of Vancouver towards the Kootenays.

Driving towards Highway 1, I wonder what's in store for me. *Allow things to be what they are*, I remind myself, as I focus on the road in front of me.

6
Go Fish

I remember you—
a coffee, black, in one hand
in the other, a smoke,
manspreading on the ragged, beige loveseat
watching the hockey game
on a small second-hand TV you brought with you when you
   moved in
to the small, one-bedroom apartment
I rent for 410 dollars a month
on the corner of Nanaimo and Graveley in Vancouver.

I remember me—
on my knees
in front of you
your dick in my mouth
and pausing for a moment,
I look up at you
and joke,
"this must be heaven to you, eh?
a coffee, a smoke, the hockey game, *and* a blowjob!"

You laugh, absentmindedly, without taking your eyes
   off the TV

you puff on your cigarette and then cheer
The Montreal Canadiens just scored.

I laugh, too and feel
connected to you, useful,
maybe even wanted,
in an empty kind of way.
And then, one weekend you go away
for three whole days.
I don't remember where you went—
who cares?
You just weren't there
And I was home
alone.

No waiting around for you to wake up until noon because
    you slept in and I didn't
and then waiting for you to have a couple cups of coffee
because you had to have it or else.
No listening to your music—funk, ska, punk—instead of my
    music—singer-songwriters, folk, roots.
No cigarette smoke seeping under the bedroom door at night
as I lay in bed trying to sleep.
No Montreal Canadiens hockey on TV
no kneeling in front of you
no obligatory blowjobs.

There was only
space,
solitude,
quiet,
me.

And Go Fish.

That weekend,
I rode my bike down to Commercial Drive, 6 blocks from my
    apartment
and rented the first film about women loving women I ever
    watched.

Go Fish was
not the kind of movie
made by straight men for straight men about lesbians.
The women in those movies were not real lesbians—
they were porn-lesbians and they didn't look like the lesbians
I used to see striding across campus
during my years as an undergraduate student at the
    University of Guelph—
Lesbians with short, buzzed haircuts, black-rimmed glasses,
    Doc Martin boots, black t-shirts, tattoos.
Go Fish was not made for guys like you.
No.

Go Fish
was a low-budget B romcom made in 1994
by lesbians
for lesbians
and women like me,
a lesbian-wanna be.

Go Fish
had actual, real
made-in-the-flesh lesbians!
different-shapes-and-sizes lesbians

butch and femme lesbians
racialized lesbians
critical-thinking lesbians
book-reading lesbians
peppermint-tea-drinking feminist lesbians
affectionate, smart, matter-of-fact, sweet, lesbians.

Lesbians who lived together and who hung out with other
    lesbians
who talked about lesbian culture, feminism, and
    stereotypes
who were rejected by their parents and adopted by their
    lesbian friends
who lived real lives, dated, and joked about trimming their
    fingernails before having sex
and, lesbians who were in love.

I was riveted.
I laughed.
I felt hopeful.
I felt seen.
I felt longing
all the way to the end
and through the credits as a song played—
"Show me a window," she sang.

Go Fish was
a world I wanted to be a part of—
a world with choice
a world of possibility
a world where I could fit.

Go Fish was
a spark,
a glimmer,
a window.

7
A revelation

I remember waking up beside you for the first time
opening my eyes to the first light of dawn
and through the open window Sentinel Mountain stood
    against a sapphire sky
and you and I lay together on my futon mattress
on the floor of my wood-paneled bedroom
in a mobile home in Pass Creek, British Columbia
my naked body curled around yours while you slept
the spring breeze wafting in over our bodies
the smell of something earthy and promising.

I remember waking up from a dream, a waking dream
my senses stirring and my body coming alive to something—
something that finally made sense.

This is what it feels like
to love a woman.

8
The night we watched *The Puppy Episode*

Content warning: This story contains details of queerphobic violence.

It is springtime in the year 2000, April to be exact. Grasses, yellow and tired from being buried under snow for nearly five months, are unfurling and waking up again. Each morning, the snowline slowly recedes up the mountainside above Norn's Creek Falls, which spills into Pass Creek, flowing southward. Pass Creek rushes and roils with the winter snowmelt, and the smell of earthen, fresh air, foretells a world reborn anew.

I drive south on Pass Creek Road, a narrow, paved road that winds through a valley meadow between Sentinel Mountain to the east and an unnamed mountain to the west. I turn the radio up and roll the window down in my 1994 maroon Ford Ranger pickup, feeling the wind on my face. It's Friday night of the Easter long weekend, and I'm heading to my girlfriend's house in town.

I am 29 years old, and I live in Castlegar, a small pulp mill town in the Selkirk Mountains in the West Kootenays, a region in the southeastern corner of British Columbia. Castlegar sits at the confluence of the Kootenay and Columbia Rivers. The town was named after a village in County Galway in Ireland by Edward Mahon, an Irish immigrant who moved to the area in 1890. "Castlegar" comes from a Gaelic phrase, *caisleán gearr*, or "short castle," perhaps in reference to the modestly sized Sentinel Mountain sitting at the northeast end of town.

When the pulp mill is converting wood into wood pulp—kraft-pulping—the mill belches out great, swollen, white plumes, and the odour of sulphur hangs in the air around the town. Most people hate that smell, but not me. I love it. It reminds me that I left the big city of Vancouver, a seven-hour drive westward along Highway 3 over three mountain passes, to move here. It reminds me that I quit a drug addiction and left an unfulfilling relationship with a man. It reminds me that I live far away from the conservative world I grew up in back in Ontario. It reminds me that I can decide for myself who I want to be and who I want to become. To me, that pulp mill odour smells like freedom.

I'm in the second semester of a one-year teacher education program at Selkirk College. Along with me, there are 39 other teacher candidates in the program, and we are all out on our teaching practicums, working in various local schools. I'm doing my practicum in a grade six class in a local elementary school on 7th Avenue in Castlegar called Twin Rivers Elementary School. Jack Kinakin is the classroom teacher and my teaching supervisor.

When Jack and I talk after school about our teaching, sometimes, he mentions his wife. They come from a Russian background like a lot of people who live in the Kootenays. His wife makes great perogies and borscht from scratch he tells me. He says I should come for dinner sometime. That would be great, I say. I love perogies and borscht.

I don't mention Danny.

Danny is my girlfriend. She lives in town with her parents. Daniela, her full name, means "God is my judge," which seems ironic since Danny's parents, Catholics, probably didn't anticipate having a daughter who is gay. Her mom is a round, reserved woman with short, curly grey hair and glasses. Danny's father is slight, white-haired, and quiet. Part of a sizeable Portuguese community in Castlegar, Danny's parents immigrated in the 1970's from the Azores Islands when Danny was three years old.

When I go to Danny's house to visit her, her parents speak Portuguese. They don't speak to me; they don't even greet me when I come in the house. They don't say a word to either of us about how I occasionally stay overnight and sleep in Danny's bedroom with her. They act as though I'm not there, and I don't know how to start a conversation with either of them. *At least they aren't outwardly hostile towards me,* I tell myself. I feel like I am lucky that I'm at least tolerated by my partner's family.

I pull up to their house—a modest white stucco two-storey with an orange clay tile roof—and park behind a gleaming red sports car out front on the street. One of Danny's three brothers, Antonio, whom I've never met, is home for the long weekend. He's visiting from Calgary, Alberta, an eight-hour drive from Castlegar.

Turning off the engine, I sit in my truck for a moment. *What is he going to think about his sister having a girlfriend? What's he going to think about his sister's girlfriend staying overnight?*

I leave the keys in a compartment in the dashboard like I always do, and walk up the driveway through the wrought iron gate. The entire front yard comprises a large plot of dark, brown soil. Come summer, that soil will burst with red, pink, and white roses, purple lavender, lettuce, fava beans, green beans, zucchini, butternut squash, tomatoes, onions, and garlic.

Through the open garage, a door opens at the top of a short set of stairs leading into the house. A hefty man appears, dressed in a ball cap, jeans, and a tight, white t-shirt. His neck is swollen and thick, like he takes steroids, and his pectoral muscles swell under his t-shirt. As he fumbles with his keys in his pocket, his biceps bulge.

"Hi, I'm Kate," I say. *This must be Antonio,* I guess silently.

He doesn't make eye contact with me but instead, strides down the stairs, brushing past me. The hair on the back of my neck stands up. Mumbling something unintelligible, he heads to his car, opens the door, gets in, and slams it shut. The engine roars to life and his car peels away from the shoulder of the road. Gravel spews out from under his car tires.

I turn back around to the open doorway. Danny is standing there in blue Levi's and a light grey hoodie. Her unruly mop of shiny chestnut curls—buzzed short around her ears and neck—is stuffed under a black, backwards ball cap. She has olive skin, a smooth, chiselled jawline, and angular shoulders.

"Hey, there!" she says to me, waving me inside. When she smiles, a tiny, crooked fang peeks out from a row of milky teeth. Her big, dark brown eyes crinkle at the edges behind wire-framed glasses. Seeing her makes me feel better. I want to hug her, but I remember where I am. Instead, I let out a sigh as I walk up the stairs and into the house. The scent of cooking garlic, onions, and tomatoes wafts out of the kitchen. Danny's mom is stirring tomato sauce on the stove. She doesn't turn around to say hello.

"How was work?" I ask Danny. Bending over to untie and remove my shoes, I place them, side by side, on the black rubber shoe mat by the door.

"Oh fine, you know, the usual. I ordered some more Sleater-Kinney and Dido today. Oh, and Dot Allison. PJ Harvey has a new album coming out soon. I want to check it out. *Stories from the City, Stories from the Sea.*"

"Great," I say.

I'm more interested in folk music, but I think it's cool Danny that works at the local music shop in town.

Digging into the pocket of my jacket, I pull out a small Tupperware container, and hang my jacket in the closet.

"Look," I whisper impishly, my eyes flashing at her. "I brought a pot brownie for us."

Danny shakes her head at me and smirks. She motions for me to follow her and we bound up the pale green carpeted stairs. Her mom clears her throat in the kitchen.

Danny opens the door onto the deck on the top of their roof, and we walk outside. Sitting beside each other on the wooden picnic table, we face the dark green coniferous forest that blankets the hill rising above the rooftops across the road. The air smells like trees—cedar, hemlock, pine, fir, and spruce. Danny opens a pack of Canadian Classics. She pulls a cigarette out and puts it between her lips. Flicking open the lid of a Zippo lighter with her thumb, she lights up, snaps the Zippo lid closed, and puts it back in the pocket of her jeans. She moves a small black plastic ashtray on the table within reach and breathes in deeply.

I wish Danny didn't smoke. Even though she's kind of sexy when she does. When I dreamed of having a girlfriend before I met her, I imagined myself with one of those hippie, outdoorsy types of women. A granola dyke, maybe? But a butchy kind of granola dyke. Somebody who hikes, cycles, camps, rock-climbs, and kayaks. Somebody who eats tofu and vegetables out of a large bowl with colourfully painted chopsticks, makes homemade soup and vegetarian chili with textured vegetable protein, sprinkles nutritional yeast on her popcorn, uses handmade soap, and shops at health food stores. Someone who lives in a cabin with a wood stove and chops her own kindling and firewood. Someone who doesn't drink or do drugs—hard drugs, at least. And someone would never consider smoking.

But mostly, I wish Danny didn't smoke because I'm still trying to quit.

I grab the lit cigarette from her fingers and take a puff. Smoke fills my lungs and I feel rebellious. Being with Danny makes me feel rebellious. People in my hometown would be surprised if they knew I was a lesbian. People in this small pulp mill town in the interior of British Columbia would be surprised if they knew there were two lesbians like us living among them.

"We should live in Nelson," I muse as I blow cigarette smoke out between my lips. "We would fit in better in Nelson. At least there are lesbians there."

Nelson is a small city down the highway about 45 minutes. There are artists and musicians, and snowboarders, ski bums, and climbers. And, hippie outdoorsy butchy granola dyke lesbians.

Danny grabs my arms and draws me to her body. She kisses me quickly on the mouth. I catch the scent of cigarette smoke and Bounce dryer sheets.

I pull away from her and look her in the eyes.

"Your brother isn't very friendly. He totally ignored me as he walked past me to his car. Is he always like that or is he homophobic?"

"Oh, never mind him!" She waves her hand dismissively in the air beside her head as if she's swatting at a pesky mosquito. "Tony's an ass, but he's harmless. Besides, he's gone out drinking to the bar with some old buddies from school. We'll be asleep before he gets back."

I feel relieved knowing he's out for the night.

"C'mon. Let's go watch that re-run!" We are going to watch *The Puppy Episode*, a re-run of the sitcom, *Ellen*. The show's protagonist, Ellen Morgan, is played by Ellen DeGeneres. Danny tells me that during this episode, Ellen comes out, revealing to her love interest, Susan, that she is gay. American actor Laura Dern plays Susan. It's the first time in TV history that a woman comes out on a national television show as a lesbian. Danny crushes out her cigarette in the ashtray and grabs my hand. We hop off the picnic table and head inside to her bedroom.

Picking up the remote from her bedside table, she flips on the TV in her room. She turns the channel to *Ellen*.

Danny says to me excitedly, "I can't wait for you to see it."

"But, I don't get it," I say, confused. "Why is it called *The Puppy Episode* if it's not about puppies?"

"Oh, because it's a code," she explains. "The TV network wanted the plot and Ellen's coming out to be kept a secret, you know? They called it *The Puppy Episode* because they didn't want to give anything away before it aired."

"Okay, got it," I reply as I sit back on her single bed. I don't own a TV, so I have never seen *Ellen* before. I am excited to see a real-life lesbian portray a lesbian character on TV.

Danny closes her bedroom door and scrambles onto the bed beside me. I open the small Tupperware container and fish out the pot brownie, dividing it in half. I give her a piece. We each pop a piece of brownie into our mouths, pull the comforter up around our bodies, and nestle back against the wall together. I put my head on her shoulder, and we begin to watch the show.

Near the end, Ellen is at the airport, saying goodbye to a friend who was in town visiting. Then, she runs into Susan, a gay woman Ellen met through a friend. People are milling about, standing in groups chatting, sitting in chairs against the wall, waiting to board their flights.

Ellen turns serious and tells Susan she wants to talk to her. My body is humming from the pot brownie.

Ellen stutters and moans, struggling to say something to Susan. Susan smiles and nods at Ellen expectantly, as if coaxing the words out of her. Ellen can't bring herself to look Susan in the eye. Instead, she paces around Susan, talking to herself, with her back to Susan.

Susan nods her head, grinning, as if sensing what Ellen is about to say. Then, she grimaces, realizing how much anguish Ellen is experiencing.

Finally, Ellen forces a breath from her mouth and shakes her head. She leans over the announcer's microphone balanced on the podium between them and proclaims, "Susan… I'm gay."

Ellen's confession echoes over the loudspeaker for everyone at the airport gate to hear. The audience erupts with uproarious laughter and then hoots and hollers, whistles and claps. My heart swells in my chest. I laugh too.

Stunned, Ellen and Susan turn to look around the room. Everyone is staring at them. They turn to face one another again. They smirk knowingly. Then, beaming at Ellen, Susan reaches her arms out toward her, and they embrace. The audience is frenzied with cheering and applause.

Tears sting my eyes and spill down my cheeks. I quickly wipe them away with the back of my hand. I clutch Danny's arm, embarrassed that I'm crying.

"It's great, isn't it?" She squeezes my knee.

"Yeah." I sniff, feeling warm inside.

"So great. It's so cool to see that on TV. To see a show with a lesbian in it who plays a lead role? And, she's happy? And funny? Wow."

After *The Puppy Episode*, Danny tells me that hate mail poured into the offices at ABC. She says that large companies pulled their advertising from the show. Well-known American evangelists publicly denounced Ellen and the show and circulated letters which thousands of churchgoers signed saying that being gay was an abomination. Death threats were posted on the front door of Ellen's home. ABC Studios received a bomb threat and then they cancelled the show a year later due to low ratings.

"That's terrible. God, people are so homophobic. I don't get it," I say, knowing that Ellen's career nosedived since that episode.

"At least she still has Anne," I point out, referring to Ellen's girlfriend, Anne Heche.

"I wonder when it will be safe for all gay people to be out in public, at our jobs, with our families. Everywhere." Danny says, fluffing the pillows, getting under the covers. I think about how Danny's parents don't acknowledge our relationship. And how I'm not out to my teaching practicum supervisor, Jack. And all the times I automatically plan quick escape routes in my head when I'm walking down the street with Danny in case some of the straight guys who stare at us decide they want to teach us a lesson.

"Yeah, and safe to even talk about it. Say the word 'lesbian' around straight people and not worry about how they will respond," I say, getting into bed beside her.

"Like, I wonder if people will ever stop caring about who other people sleep with. Stop hating us, you know?" Lying down on my side, I wrap my arm across her chest.

"Yeah," she murmurs, her eyes closed. I close my eyes, too, and drift off.

****

Hours later, the deep, garbled voice of a man drones somewhere above me. Then, it stops. I must be dreaming. Danny groans quietly beside me.

Then, I hear the voice again. Louder this time. I open my eyes. I see the outline of Antonio's brawny frame standing over Danny and me in the dark. The hallway light spills into the bedroom. I glance quickly at Danny's digital clock radio. 2 a.m.

I'm not dreaming.

Antonio growls something but I can't make out what he says.

"What?" I mumble, half-asleep.

"I said, 'get the fuck up, you cunt-licking bitches,'" he demands, slurring.

My heart lurches against my ribs. My scalp prickles. I begin to register what is happening and sit up.

Danny opens her eyes and sees Antonio. She props herself up on her elbow.

"Tony, what the hell?" She reaches for her glasses on the bedside table. "Get out of here!"

Antonio points a thick finger at Danny. In hallway light, I can see the curve of his deltoid muscle under the sleeve of his t-shirt.

"Shut up, Daniella." He looks at me. "Hurry up. I'll wait for you both downstairs."

His bulky frame disappears from the doorframe. Heavy footsteps trudge down the stairs. Danny lies back down and pulls the comforter up around her.

I pull her arm.

"Dan. C'mon!" I hiss. I know better than to argue with a drunk, angry man in the middle of the night. Especially one as big as Danny's brother.

"Just do what he says."

I feel hazy from the pot brownie. My hands shake as I reach for my jeans and sweatshirt piled on the floor. *Why haven't Danny's parents come out of their bedroom to see what's going on? Why am I so afraid of waking them up to ask for help? Where are Danny and I going to go at two in the morning? What if we don't even make it out the door because Antonio does something more than threaten us?*

I stand up and struggle into my clothes. Danny rolls out of bed and pulls her clothes on. She grabs her ballcap and slaps it on her head. Grabbing her wallet from the desk, she crams it into her pocket.

Out in the lit hallway, I can see Antonio down below, at the bottom of the stairs, sitting at the kitchen table. Danny treads down the stairs ahead of me. I follow. Antonio rises to his feet. Burly and muscular, he puffs his chest out.

"You need to leave. Now. You dykes are not welcome in this house."

I put on my shoes and grab my jacket from the closet.

Danny tries to reason with him. "C'mon, Tony. What are you talking about? You're drunk and you're being totally unreasonable. It's the middle of the night. We can talk in the morning."

His jugular vein bulges on his thick neck. Anger radiates off him.

"Jesus fucking Christ, Daniela. You're not listening to me. Why are you not listening to me, you fucking dyke?"

"Dan, let's go!" I plead through clenched teeth, yanking on her arm. I open the door and start down the stairs and sprint along the path through the front yard toward my truck. I hear Antonio yelling behind me. I stop and look back to see him and Danny arguing on the stairs.

"You goddamn queers disgust me. You're an embarrassment to Mom and Dad. To this town. Get the fuck out of here!" He shoves her down the stairs. "Get out!"

My heart hammers the inside of my ribcage. "Dan! Let's go!" I yell at her again, running toward the truck. I jump into the driver's side. Reaching into the comparment in the dashboard, I fumble with the keys and jam the truck key into the ignition. The passenger door opens and Danny lurches in beside me.

"Lock the door!" I insist, turning the key. The engine rumbles to life. Then, an ear-splitting crack fills the cab. Glass shatters, spraying all over Danny and me, hitting the side of my face. I scream. Antonio's fist appears through the broken passenger-side window. A pile of tempered glass sits in Danny's lap. As I stomp on the gas pedal, we roar away from the curb.

"Holy fuck, Dan!" I say, my voice quivering. "I don't know where we're going. Where are we going? It's after two in the morning."

My brain feels cloudy, but my body is saturated with adrenaline.

"We can go to Carlos' place."

"Are you sure?" I ask, unconvinced. I've never met Carlos but given what just happened with Antonio, I'm not sure if it's a good idea to go to her other brother's house.

"Yeah, he and Ange are cool," she reassures me. I have no choice but to trust her.

Giving me directions to get to Carlos and Angela's house, she pulls a cigarette from a half-empty pack on the dash and rummages in the pocket of her jeans for her Zippo. I look over and see her hands tremble as she lights her cigarette and takes a lungful of smoke.

"Holy shit, that was crazy. Tony's crazy," Danny whistles.

She rolls the window down. I roll mine down. The fresh air feels good on my face.

As I drive, my mind races. *What if a cop pulls us over and I get arrested for driving stoned and end up in jail? What will Jack, my classroom supervisor at Twin Rivers Elementary School think when he finds out I have a girlfriend? What will the students and parents say when they find out there has been a lesbian in their school? What if someone complains and I get kicked out of the teacher education program? Do stories like this end up in the local news? What if the whole town finds out that Danny and I are lesbians? What if we have to move somewhere far away because everywhere we go in Castlegar, people hate us? What will become of me if I can't earn a living teaching? What will I do with my life? What will happen to Danny and me?*

A hot flush creeps up my neck and my forehead breaks out in beads of sweat.

A few minutes later, we arrive at Carlos and Angela's. We slip out of the truck and go to the front door. Danny knocks. I shift my weight from one foot to the other, peering over my shoulder in the dark, worried that Antonio might have followed us. Danny knocks again, harder this time. We wait. The night air is chilly.

The door opens and a large, round, balding man in sweatpants and an oversized t-shirt stands before us.

"Daniela," he says, surprised. He looks at me and then back at Danny. "What…what are you doing here?"

"Can you let us in? We were at Mom and Dad's, and Tony came back from the bar drunk and kicked us out of the house," she explains hastily.

"What?" Carlos looks baffled for a minute. Then, his expression changes to one of recognition. "Oh shit. That motherfucker. Yeah, come in, come in." He ushers us inside, closes the door behind us, and shoves the deadbolt in place, locking it. Relief washes over me.

"This is Kate," Danny says to Carlos.

"This is Carlos," she says to me, nodding at her brother.

"Hi. Thanks for letting us in," I say to Carlos. "Sorry to bother you in the middle of the night."

"Come sit down. I'll make you some coffee." Carlos motions to a small round kitchen table with four wooden chairs.

We sit down. He stands at the kitchen counter with his back turned to us as he fills the drip coffee maker with water and coffee grounds. I hear a door open down the hallway. A tall, plump woman in fuzzy bunny slippers emerges from the darkness and shuffles into the kitchen. A lilac-coloured terry cloth robe, open at the front, drapes haphazardly over her round body revealing a light pink nightgown underneath speckled with tiny flowers and little ruffles down the front.

"Carlos? Danny?" She rubs her eyes. "What the hell is goin' on?" She squints at me.

"Sorry about waking you up, Ange. You remember Kate, my girlfriend? You met at Timmy's a couple of months ago," Danny answers.

"Oh yeah. Hi," Angela says as she plunks herself down in a chair and heaves her legs under the table. Her round face is kind and a bit haggard.

"Hi, Angela," I say. "I'm sorry we woke you up."

I remember meeting Angela at the take-out window at Tim Horton's—a chain of cafés that sells drip coffee and donuts. Wearing a dark brown polyester uniform, her bleached blonde hair was stuffed into a hairnet that puffed out under a matching dark brown visor. I remember her long, manicured, bright, fuchsia fingernails as she opened the take-out window to pass us our coffee in paper cups with plastic lids.

Angela pulls a mauve-coloured hair elastic off her wrist. Running pointy, frosted-pink fingernails through her platinum hair—exposing dark brown roots underneath—she tugs it all back into a sloppy ponytail. Fishing a cigarette out from a pack of Benson and Hedges menthol on the kitchen table, she thrusts it between her lips and lights it. I marvel at how she can do anything with those extensive fingernails. I look down at my nails, all chewed and frayed.

Angela inhales and blows smoke over her shoulder.

"Okay," she says as she rests her cigarette on the edge of a glass ashtray in the middle of the table. She squints at Danny and me.

"What the hell are you two doin' here at this hour?" She looks at Carlos. "Is someone going to tell me what happened?"

Danny and I look at each other. Then, we take turns describing what happened with Antonio. When we are done, Angela sits back.

"For fuck's sakes!" Cigarette smoke shoots out of her nostrils. "What an asshole. It's 2000, Tony. Get over it."

She taps her cigarette with a frosted-pink fingernail. Greyish-white ash falls into the ashtray.

"We have to call the cops and report this."

Carlos brings four cups of coffee to the table. He also sets down a carton of cream, a small dish of sugar cubes, and four teaspoons.

"I agree," he says.

"Me too," I say. We all turn and look at Danny expectantly.

"Yeah, I guess we should. It's weird. He's my brother." Danny looks at Carlos. "Our brother."

"I know," Carlos sighs.

Angela puts down her cigarette and looks at Danny.

"It's wrong, what he did," she says.

"I know, I know," Danny agrees, looking at the floor.

"Besides," Angela tosses her head, "he's a dick anyway. Someone needs to put him in his place," she declares hoarsely.

She shifts her rump in her chair, pulls her robe closed around her fleshy frame, and takes a slurp of coffee.

"It's homophobia. A hate crime." I assert. "Should I call?"

"Right. Yeah," Carlos says. He hands me the cordless phone. I call 911. A woman's voice answers.

"RCMP[3], Castlegar detachment. How may I direct your call?"

Five hours later, an RCMP car pulls up behind my truck in front of Carlos and Angela's house. I joke sarcastically that cops must be busy in small towns like Castlegar on long weekends. Danny smiles weakly. Carlos frowns and shakes his head.

"Pathetic." Angela snorts and lights up another cigarette.

Danny and I walk out the front door to greet the police. Sunlight begins to spread down the sides of the trees. A robin hops about on the front lawn, eyeing the grass for a worm to yank from the soil. At least the effects of the pot brownie have worn off, but I feel drained from being up most of the night.

The woman and man in RCMP uniforms ask us for our names, addresses, and phone numbers. Then, as the woman writes notes in a small pad of paper, she asks us to tell them what happened. She then motions to my truck and requests to look it over. We walk over to my truck. That's when I notice all four tires are flat.

"What the hell? The tires are flat! How did…?" My anxiety changes to anger. I turn to Danny.

"Either he did that before we left your parents', or he figured we were here and came over and did it while we were inside."

I think about how much money it's going to cost me to repair my truck. My stomach churns. As a student in teacher's college, money is very tight. It doesn't occur to me that I could ask Danny or her parents to help pay for the damages, let alone expect that Antonio will.

Danny draws a deep breath. "Shit. What a bastard," she mutters, shaking her head.

Taking notes, the police walk around the truck. They crouch down to examine each tire. They assess where the window used to be in the passenger side door. As they open the passenger door to look inside the cab, tiny, cube-shaped chunks of glass fall to the ground from the window frame. Hundreds of small fragments of glass lie on the bench seat, the floor, and the dashboard. The policewoman jots down more notes.

"Well, that's about it," she says, flipping her pad of paper closed. She looks at us. "You two need to come down to the station and make a statement. Can you do that this morning?"

"Yes," says Danny, exhaling.

"Then what?" I ask.

"We will put a province-wide warrant out for his arrest," the policeman informs us.

"What does that mean exactly?" I ask. "Antonio lives in Calgary, so…?"

Looking at his watch, the policeman cuts me off.

"It means that he can be arrested when he's in the province, in BC. But once he crosses the border and goes back home to Calgary, we can't arrest him."

Danny says, "Well, he's still over at my parents' house. He drives a red sports car. A Nissan," she adds quickly.

The policeman jingles his keys in his hand. "We'll go and see," he responds abruptly.

He turns around and walks towards the police car.

"See you at the station," the policewoman smiles at us and gets in the car, rolling down the window. "It's Saturday, so make sure to come before we close at 4 p.m."

The police pull away from the curb. Turning left at the stop sign at the end of the road, the opposite direction from the street where Danny's parents live, the car disappears.

Later that morning, after we have breakfast with Carlos and Angela, I call a tow truck company to come and take my truck to a garage for repairs. I book a rental car for a few days. Angela drives Danny and me to the car rental company, and then Danny and I drive to the police station. There is a different policewoman there who takes our statement.

"Did they bring him to the station for questioning?" I ask.

"It says here that they went to the house, but there was no red Nissan in the driveway."

"Did they go up and knock on the door to see if they could find out where he was?" I press her.

She smiles weakly. "I'm sorry, ma'am. It looks like they weren't able to track down the suspect."

I look at Danny.

"So, that's it? He just gets to walk away from what he did?" I probe. Danny shakes her head.

"I'm sorry, ma'am," she repeats. "It says here they have reason to believe he's gone back to Alberta. We did the best we could."

"Thanks," Danny responds.

We leave the police station and drive up the winding road to the place I'm renting in Pass Creek.

On Monday morning, I drop Danny off at the music store and drive to Twin Rivers Elementary School. I manoeuvre the rental car into a staff parking space in front of the school. My heart thumps in my chest as I sling my bag of teaching supplies over my shoulder and walk toward the school.

When I get to the front door, I put my hand on the door handle. Raising my head, I take a large gulp of air into my lungs, square my shoulders, open the door, and walk inside. The halls are empty; the bell doesn't ring for another hour. I pace down the hall toward the grade six classroom. The lights are on. Thoughts about what I'm going to say to Jack stampede through my mind.

When I walk in, he is writing on the blackboard.

"Hi, Jack," I say.

He turns to face me.

"Ms Hancock," he beams. "How are you today? Did you have a good long weekend?"

"I'm great, thanks, Jack." I smile and nod, setting down my bag on one of the students' desks.

"My weekend was pretty good. How about you?"

9
Wildhorse Creek Road

Jonah and I are teachers at a high school in Midway, a tiny rural town in southern British Columbia. We rent a double-wide, beige and brown aluminum-sided mobile home on an 800-acre ranch, a couple of kilometers out of town. Jonah was born half an hour down the road in Grand Forks and comes from a Russian family. He is tall, good-looking, athletic, and musical. He has a warm smile and a beautiful, deep voice with a booming laugh, and he laughs at my jokes. And, he makes great spaghetti sauce.

Within six months of our relationship, I try to convince Jonah we should have a child together. I am surprised at this sudden urge. Raising children was never something I wanted. I never yearned to have a baby grow inside my body nor could I imagine one exiting my body. That has always felt unfathomable, not to mention, it seems so painful. I always used to cringe thinking about it. Yet, now, here I am.

"I'm 30 years old. It's time," I plead.

"Babe, I don't want to," he tells me, holding my hand. "One child is enough for me."

Jonah has a 9-year-old daughter, Joy, who we see on weekends. She lives with her mom in Kelowna, a couple of hours away. I feel a twinge of jealousy that Jonah has a child with another woman, but I dismiss it. Joy's a great kid and I marvel at all the ways that Jonah loves her.

Within two weeks, I forget why I ever wanted a child in the first place. *Must have been a phase,* I think to myself.

At the end of the school year, Jonah and I decide to quit our teaching jobs and leave Midway. Neither of us is happy here.

"Even though it's beautiful here, I'm glad we're leaving this place," I say to Jonah as, one last time, we drive up the laneway from our rented mobile home onto Highway 3. My Ford Ranger pick-up truck is stuffed to the brim with our belongings.

"It's just too conservative here," I declare, as I survey the rolling hills and sprawling ranchland passing by us along the highway. Jonah agrees.

As I breathe in the warm summer air swirling in through the open windows, I think about Danny. She and I were still dating when I landed my first teaching job in Midway. Trouble is, it was hard being gay here.

During my first year teaching in Midway, I kept my personal life and my relationship with Danny to myself—especially in the staffroom, when all the other straight teachers were talking about their husbands and wives and families. On weekends, I didn't socialize with them. I didn't want to have to field personal questions or accidentally say something that would tip them off. If word got out here that my partner was a woman, I don't know what would happen to me.

Instead, after the bell rang each Friday, I got in my truck and drove nearly two hours back to Castlegar to see Danny. Then, each Sunday afternoon, I drove back to Midway and resumed my life as a closeted queer teacher.

At the end of my first year in Midway, Danny and I split up. It wasn't working for a range of reasons, one of which was the internalized homophobia that I can't shake. Jonah—the physical education teacher at the school— feels like a safe, easy place to land after I end things with Danny.

When Jonah and I first start dating, I tell him about Danny. I tell him about the women I made out with in gay bars and at women's music festivals. He doesn't seem to care, and he doesn't make offensive sexual comments that some straight men sometimes make about lesbians. He's just a warm-hearted, easy-going guy.

When Jonah moves into the double-wide trailer with me, my social life in Midway comes alive. We spend time with the other teachers. We host parties at our house and get invited to parties hosted by our co-workers. We go for beers after work at the local pub and gossip about the school administrators. We play baseball in a local rec league. I am struck by how easy my life suddenly becomes. My desire for women fades into the background, and I am relieved.

But, as Jonah and I begin planning to leave Midway and I think about moving back to the Kootenays with him, thoughts of meeting a woman start creeping back into my mind. I begin daydreaming about how we would meet, what we might do on dates, and what our life together could look like.

A warm hand closes over mine on the seat beside me, pulling me out of my reverie. I look over at Jonah and smile. He's really sweet, I think. I pull my hand away and crank up the Macy Gray CD in the truck stereo. Then, reaching for his hand again, I focus on the road ahead of us.

We find a mobile home to rent in Slocan Park, a small unincorporated village in the Slocan Valley not far from Castlegar. Jonah gets a job as a substitute teacher with the Kootenay-Columbia District School Board. I get a job as a teacher at a private school, called the Valican Whole. It's a few minutes up the road and it's organized and run by the parents whose children are the students. Many of the parents grow marijuana for a living.

Jonah and I have fun together. We ride our bikes, hike and camp in the backcountry, snowboard at the local ski hills, canoe on Slocan Lake, float down the Slocan River in the summer in black rubber inner tubes, drink beer, play our guitars, and laugh. We have two dogs and a cute cat. His daughter, Joy, visits us every two weeks for the weekend. When I am with him, I feel content.

One day, I come home after walking the dogs and Jonah is out. Grabbing a glass of water, I go into our home office. I start my summer job tomorrow and I have to check my email account once more before I leave for six weeks.

Sitting down on the swivel chair at the desk, I move the arrow to the middle of the black screen of the monitor of our desktop computer and click on the mouse to revive the window. It flashes open to an image of a young woman perched on the edge of a bed. Dry shoulder-length bleached blonde hair sprouts from dark brown roots at her scalp and hangs down beside her face.

Her large breasts are stuffed into an underwire white lace bra. She looks at the camera. Her eyes seem empty. My heart thumps. My esophagus tightens. I swallow.

My hand hovers over the "play" button. I inhale sharply and press my finger down on the mouse. It clicks and the video rolls. A sleazy male voice delivers directions from behind the Handycam. She follows his instructions.

The young woman looks up at the camera through made-up eyelashes. She puts her hand between her legs, rubbing herself.

Jonah's been watching porn? And, homemade porn? Really?

She twirls strands of hair around one finger and talks in a baby voice to the man behind the camera. She has a weak smile on her round, grey face. My stomach twists as I watch. Anger churns inside me.

Fuck you, Jonah. She isn't even good-looking, and she looks like she uses cheap conditioner!

Then, a weight presses on my insides. I wonder if the young woman on my computer screen feels stuck. Stuck in the belief that the only option she has is to lie on a bed in front of some nauseating guy with a Handycam doing whatever he tells her to do. That she might never find a career that feels exciting and motivating and pays her well. That she doesn't know how to create a life for herself that fills her with joy.

I feel stuck. Stuck in this relationship with Jonah. Stuck in the worry that I will never find someone I trust enough to tell them about the complicated history I have with my body and with sex and that I don't always want to spread my legs for them just because they want me to. That I might never find a woman to love and who will love me back. That I don't know how to create a life for myself that fills me with joy.

Other than the cheap porn thing, Jonah is a nice guy. We make a great couple. But, he's still a guy.

He's just like all the rest of them, I think bitterly.

I wonder what my friends will say when I tell them about this. *What kind of feminist woman has a boyfriend who watches porn, especially behind her back??* I snort.

Then, an idea flashes into my mind.

The porn is my way out. It's the only way I can get out of an otherwise functional, loving relationship. It's the only way I can free myself up and make space in my life to meet a woman.

I declare out loud to myself, "It's over. I just can't be with a man who watches this sexist crap."

When Jonah gets home later, we fight.

"You left the internet open on the desktop." I cross my arms in front of my chest.

"I didn't realize you were into shit porn."

Jonah's eyes widen and his mouth drops open.

"How could you? It's so gross!" I yell.

"We haven't had sex for a year, Kate!" he bellows. "A whole year."

His chest puffs up. His broad shoulders square.

For an instant, I feel afraid. Then, the heat of humiliation spreads across my cheeks.

"We never talk about it," he throws his hands up in the air. "What am I supposed to do?"

An instinct to fight rises inside me. Rage churns in my chest.

"I thought you were different from the other guys!" I shout.

Jonah's eyebrows knit together, his chest deflates, and his shoulders slump.

"I can't be with someone who watches porn," I announce. "And crap homemade porn, at that."

I spin around and storm down the narrow trailer corridor back to our bedroom and throw myself on the bed beside a pile of clothes. My heart aches. As tears sting my eyes, I feel myself sinking into shame. Questions circle around in my mind, like they have so many times before.

Why can't I figure out how to keep things together? Why can't I find someone who I can stay with for longer than two years? Why do I fail at every relationship? What's wrong with me? What am I going to do now?

This is such bad timing. I leave tomorrow for my summer job, and I'm still not done packing. Sitting up, I begin folding t-shirts and shorts from the pile of clothes on the bed. I place them neatly in my large, multi-day backpack. I'll be gone for most of the summer—six weeks in total. I'm a field coordinator for a youth summer leadership program with 12 youth and my new co-worker, Miles. We'll be doing community projects and learning about the environment, the people, and the history of the places we visit along the great Columbia River, which weaves through the Kootenays, down through Washington and Oregon, before emptying out into the Pacific Ocean at Portland.

The next morning, Jonah and I talk.

Putting his hand on mine, Jonah says, "Let's figure this out at the end of the summer, Kate. I'm sorry," he offers, his eyes dim.

"Yeah, that's a good idea," I agree, quietly. Tears pool behind my eyelids. "I'm sorry, too."

I hear a vehicle coming up the driveway and then a horn. I wipe my eyes with the back of my hand and jump up. Miles just pulled up in the large passenger van we'll be driving around the Kootenays all summer. After hugging Jonah goodbye, I walk outside to the van, throw my backpack in the back, and jump into the passenger side.

"Hey, Kate! You ready?" He flashes me a friendly smile. I remember that smile from when we first met during the group interview for this job.

"Sure am! Let's get out of here!" I reply, smiling back, ready to leave behind my life for a few weeks.

Miles reverses down the driveway, onto the road, and we drive away, heading to Nelson to pick up the youth and start our summer together.

As we wind along the road toward the junction at the highway that will take us to Nelson, I sneak a look at Miles. He is 29 years old with dark, curly, brown hair, sparkly bright blue eyes, a wide grin, and a passion for the outdoors—especially rock climbing. He's easy to be with. Nonchalant and laid-back, young and unambitious. He's cute and his jokes make me laugh.

****

I lie on my side in my dark green, down mummy bag in my four-person, three-season Eureka tent, a tent I bought for camping trips with Jonah. A pair of folded up fleece pants from Mountain Equipment Co-op provides an improvised pillow under my head. My Therm-a-Rest provides some insulation and cushioning from the cool bumpy ground. Cricket songs rise into the night air as they rub their tiny legs together in the dewy grass outside my tent.

It's the end of August and autumn is coming. Small, breathy clouds swirl out my mouth against the backdrop of the dull porch light that filters through the translucent tent fly. I'm staying in the backyard at my friend, Rebecca's. She and her 8-year-old son, Oliver, live in a small house on Goose Creek Road, a dead-end, dirt road off the highway that runs between Castlegar and Nelson. A week ago, Jonah and I broke up and moved out of the mobile home we rented.

Now, I'm living in my tent—homeless, jobless, single, and broke.

And, pregnant.

Earlier that evening, I stand barefoot in Rebecca's cramped bathroom, bending over the sink in my favourite cut-off army shorts, a white tank top, and a bright orange toque I bought from a second-hand store in Nelson.

"Fuck, I can't believe this. I'm such an idiot," I murmur.

A tiny pink stripe materializes in the little window of the white plastic wand of a home pregnancy test I bought at Shoppers Drug Mart in Castlegar. Stepping backwards, I slide down the wall beside the bathtub. I pull my knees up to my chest and huddle in the corner.

"Fucking Miles," I gasp. Shame and anger flood my body. A tear traces a silent path down my cheek. Rebecca crouches down, putting her hand on my knee.

"'Fucking Miles' is right," she agrees.

"What am I talking about? This is *my* fault," I scoff. Looking at her, I smack the heel of my hand against my forehead and rest my head there.

"It's finally happened, Rebecca. After all these years of unprotected sex with men. I deserve this for messing around on Jonah."

"You don't deserve this, Kate. It happens," she replies. She squeezes my knee. "What are you going to do?"

I look at her, perplexed.

"Have an abortion, of course," I shrug. "What else would I do? You know I don't want a kid. Especially not with Miles."

I can barely take care of myself, let alone a kid, I think silently. Besides, I don't want to be tied to a guy for the rest of my life.

"Yeah," Rebecca says, standing up. "Let's make us some noodle kugel for dinner. Kugel makes everything better."

I stand up, straighten my shorts, throw the white plastic wand with the pink stripe into the wastebasket, wash my face, and follow her into the kitchen, relieved that Oliver is absorbed in afternoon cartoons in the living room. Rebecca pulls eggs out of the fridge and grabs a mixing bowl from the cupboard.

"I have to make an appointment to see my doctor to make sure I'm actually pregnant." I retrieve a mesh bag of onions from the top of the fridge and a bag of potatoes from under the sink.

"Good idea. Then you can just get it done in Nelson."

Rebecca butters a 9 × 13-inch baking pan. She turns the oven on to 350 degrees.

"At the hospital?" I crack eggs into a bowl. I think about the egg inside me that was fertilized by Miles' eager, 29-year-old sperm. I cringe. *What was I thinking?*

"Yep," she shrugs as she peels potatoes. Rebecca knows about these kinds of things. She works at a community organization in town that supports women leaving violent relationships.

"Are you going to tell Miles?"

I grate the freshly peeled potatoes into the mixing bowl and dice up a small onion.

"Yeah. I should, shouldn't I?" I whisk the eggs and onions together until the yellow mixture looks frothy and chunky. Rebecca uses a wooden spoon to mix the grated potatoes in with the onions, eggs, some salt and pepper, and a bit of oil.

"I don't know. I guess so. That fucker," she exclaims. "Didn't you use anything?"

"Rebecca, please. I've never used protection, remember?" I sigh. "Sometimes I think I'm just lucky to be alive, all the stupid stuff I've done."

"Yeah, I know. Me too," she says. "What about Jonah? Are you going to tell him?"

She dumps the contents of the bowl into the baking pan and spreads the pale-yellow concoction around. I think about how Jonah's face will look when I tell him that I got pregnant with Miles. My stomach turns.

I start washing the dishes. Wincing, I reply, "Yeah, I feel like I should tell him even though we broke up. I'm such an asshole."

"Well, you're not an asshole," she asserts, sliding the pan of kugel mixture into the oven and closing the door.

"But," she looks at me, raising her plucked eyebrows. "You do need to stop telling everyone you're a lesbian if you keep sleeping with men."

Shame slithers across my skin. My face burns. I look down at the floor.

I know I sleep with men; I've had a lot of relationships with men. But that doesn't make me straight, does it? I don't want to live with a man for the rest of my life, I know that. I had a girlfriend before I was with Jonah. I've kissed a few women. I feel more whole when I am with women, even when I'm just hanging out with my friends who are women. I want to live my life with women. I want to share a home with a woman, have a cat and maybe a dog, plant a garden, share meals together, sit on the porch, drink tea, watch the sun set, curl up with her in bed at night, read, and fall asleep beside her. Then, I want to wake up in the morning and do it all over again. Doesn't all this make me a lesbian?

What does Rebecca know anyway? Fuck her.

I wipe my hands on my shorts and use a dishtowel that has little birds printed on it to wipe the counter. Pulling the plug in the sink, I watch the dirty water swirl down the drain.

"I feel like shit," I say. "I think I just need to go to my tent and sleep."

"Really? But, what about dinner? The kugel?" Rebecca pleads.

I feel a twinge of guilt.

"I'm sorry, Bec," I say. "I can't."

"I'm sorry I said that." She puts her hand on my arm. "It's just…"

"Don't be sorry. You're probably right." The words almost get caught in my throat. I don't look at her.

"Goodnight."

"Goodnight," she sighs.

I grab my flannel shirt off the kitchen chair and walk past Oliver in the living room, sprawled out on the couch. He doesn't take his eyes off the TV. I don't bother to say "goodnight." What does he care? What does anybody care? I'm fucked.

Opening the back door, I step out onto the deck and look up at the dimming sky. I can breathe out here. I walk over to a bush behind the shed, pull down my shorts, and crouch in the tall grass to pee. I think about Jonah. I think about Miles. I think about the little thing that's attached to the inside of my uterus, growing. I wonder if it already has a spirit.

I finish peeing and stand up. I pull my shorts up and trudge over to my tent, unzip the door, and crawl inside. As I wiggle into my sleeping bag and lie down, I put my hand on my abdomen. I think about Miles and about how being with him made me forget that Jonah and I were finished and how I loved Jonah but not in the way that I should and how I didn't really have to commit to Miles because I knew it was just a rebound affair and how I just wanted one more guy to distract me from who I was.

"Oh my god," I say out loud. Bolting upright on my Therma-Rest, I cover my mouth with my hands, my sleeping bag bunched around my waist.

"I've been using men this whole time," I whisper through my fingers. "I've been sleeping with them to try and convince myself that I'm not queer."

How could this be? All this time, I had been telling myself that men use women for sex. That men were the ones who just got what they wanted from women and then threw them away. It never occurred to me that I was doing the same. That I used men to help me feel wanted and attractive, to help me fit in and feel straight. Maybe that's why I was so insistent that Jonah and I have a child within the first few months of our relationship. Maybe I was desperate to have a kid with a man because it would prove that I wasn't queer.

My shoulders shake. As sobs wrack my body, I put my hands beside me on the tent floor to steady myself. Tears run down my cheeks. It's hard to breathe.

After a few minutes, I wipe my face with the corner of my sleeping bag. The sun has gone down and the darkness is creeping in. I cinch the hood of my down bag around my head to block out the chilly air. The crickets begin singing. A warm light from Rebecca's living room window spills out onto the lawn, casting a glow into my tent.

I'm pregnant. I'm alone. I'm a lesbian.

And, I need to find a place to live.

****

The ad in the Nelson Daily News reads, "Small cabin for rent. Wood heat. 40 acres. Washing machine. Propane stove. Beside Wildhorse Creek near Ymir. $500/month. Utilities not included. Call Ashanti at 505-5443." I dial the number from Rebecca's cordless phone.

"Allo?"

"Hi, my name is Kate. I'm calling about the cabin for rent. I saw the ad in the Nelson newspaper. Is it still available?" I ask.

"Ah, oui! This is Ashanti. The cabin is still available," she tells me in a Québécois accent. She gives me directions to the cabin.

The next afternoon, I drive to Ymir, a tiny town 30 minutes from Rebecca's house. As soon as I drive up the laneway to the cabin, I know I want to live here. It's a small log building with a chimney set back off the dirt road and nestled against the evergreen forest. A hundred feet or so in front of the cabin lies a grove of aspen trees and beyond that, a field of tall, yellow grass. On the other side of the field, a homestead spreads out behind a wooden fence—a house, a small barn, and a couple of outbuildings.

A woman stands on the uncovered deck at the front of the cabin. With long brown hair that hangs down her back to her waist, she waves at me, revealing a hairy armpit. She wears flowing green cotton wrap pants that are tied up in the front, a tank top with large pink flowers on it, and brown Birkenstock sandals. She looks like a classic Kootenay hippie woman. I jump out of my truck and walk down the path to the steps of the deck. Birds are chirping in the trees beside the shed. A river burbles nearby. My heart swells. *That must be Wildhorse Creek,* I think.

"Âllo! Bienvenue! Welcome. Je m'appelle Ashanti," she says, smiling. I walk up the steps and shake her hand.

"Hi. Nice to meet you, Ashanti. I'm Kate. Thank you for letting me look at the cabin."

She invites me inside. I step through the open door and feel at home right away.

"It's an old miner's cabin that we fixed up. We built this little front area to extend the living room and we added that front deck," she explains.

The walls of the one-room cabin are dark brown logs chinked with white plaster. The floorboards are painted mustard yellow. A black cast iron wood stove stands in the middle of the room. I can already see where my couch and coffee table and chair and bookshelf will go. The kitchen area has a full-sized fridge, an oven, and a window over the double sink. Sunlight streams through the west-facing window looking out over the deck.

Motioning to the kitchen wall, Ashanti says, "Outside on the other side of this wall, there's a shed attached to the cabin where you can stack your wood. You can get a cord around here delivered for, uh, peut être, a hundred and fifty dollars. You will probably need two cords to get you through the winter."

"Great. I love wood heat," I answer. Chopping and stacking wood and building fires in wood stoves reminds me of growing up on my family's farm in Ontario.

"Come and see upstairs," she says, beckoning me up a ladder leading into a large cutout in the ceiling above. Upstairs, there's a bedroom with a sloping ceiling. The only place I can stand up straight is where the ceiling peaks in the middle of the room. A large, west-facing window looks out over the front deck, the grove of aspen trees, the field of yellow grass, the valley, and beyond that, the Bonnington Mountain Range.

Back downstairs, Ashanti agrees to rent me the cabin and I give her a cheque for the first month's rent and another one for the damage deposit. We agree that I will move in on the 15th of the month.

"Thank you, universe," I breathe out loud to myself as I drive away. I don't know how I'm going to live way out here with no job and a truck that doesn't have four-wheel drive, which is a must-have to get up and down a road like Wildhorse Creek in the wintertime. But, I don't care. I think about my upcoming appointment at the Nelson hospital to have the abortion. I think about how I can't wait to be free of the relentless thoughts about Jonah and Miles and this mess I got myself into.

A few days after moving into the cabin, I pack a small overnight bag and drive to the hospital. Rebecca meets me in the parking lot outside. We go inside and I sign in at the reception desk. After sitting in the waiting area for a few minutes, a nurse walks up and greets us and I ask her if Rebecca can come with me. The nurse agrees and escorts us through two swinging doors and down the hall.

The air smells like disinfectant. The nurse shows me to a change room, hands me a blue hospital gown, and a basket. Instructing me to place my clothes in the basket and put on the gown, she yanks the curtain across to give me privacy.

When I emerge, she takes me to a bed near the operating room door and motions for me to lie down. Rebecca takes my hand. The nurse wipes rubbing alcohol on the back of my left hand with a cotton ball and slides a needle into one of the thick blue-green veins on my hand. Taking the cap off the back of the syringe, she attaches a thin, clear IV hose to a bag of liquid and hooks the bag onto the IV pole. My hand feels like it's burning as the liquid surges into my vein. I can't tell if the tears brimming in my eyes are from the pain of the IV, the shame that's coursing through me, or both. I tell myself that I deserve it for getting pregnant.

Turning to Rebecca, the nurse says, "time to go."

I let go of Rebecca's hand.

"I will be here when you get out."

"Thanks," I smile weakly.

The nurse wheels me in through the swinging operating room door. Three people in scrubs are milling about organizing trays of medical instruments. I try not to think about what they are going to do to my body while I'm under the anesthetic. I have to trust that they are just doing their jobs. I shudder knowing that they are going to press a vacuum up against my vulva and suck the lining of my uterus out, along with the tiny, fertilized egg.

I wonder what they do with it after that? Do they just throw it in the trash with all the other hospital waste? Is my uterus lining and the tiny, fertilized egg going to rot in a massive garbage bin alongside other people's internal organs, shitty diapers, pissy medical bed pads, mounds of bloody gauze from surgeries, used maxi pads, and heaps of food scraps and plastic cutlery?

Standing over me, the anesthesiologist puts the oxygen mask over my face.

"Okay, dear. Just count backwards from ten to zero," she tells me.

"10-9-8-7-6..."

****

After the abortion, I stay at Rebecca's to recover.

Then, a couple of days later, I drive out of town, alone, towards Ymir and my cabin on Wildhorse Creek Road. As I begin the ascent up the winding dirt road, I roll down my window. The larches are starting to turn bright gold on the mountainsides. Autumn is near.

As I meander around the last corner of the road, the cabin comes into view. The west-facing bedroom window reflects the afternoon sun. The long, yellow grasses ripple in the field in front of the cabin, welcoming me back. The leaves of the aspen trees flip and flutter in the breeze like sequins, dark green, then light green, then dark green again. Pulling into the laneway, I park the truck, pick up my duffle bag, and go inside.

I fill the kettle up with water, light the element on the stove with a match, and set the kettle down on the ring of blue flame. A warm September draught floats in through the window I open over the sink. I climb the ladder and go into my bedroom. I change into my army shorts and white tank top. I flop onto the king-sized mattress that Jonah and I bought when we first moved in together, looking up at the ceiling. I remember how he came to visit me one night at Rebecca's and how we sat in my tent in the backyard. And how he cried when I told him I was pregnant. And how I cried knowing I had hurt him. Knowing I had been selfish and reckless and had messed up both of our lives for a while.

Climbing down the ladder, I walk over to the stove, remove the whistling kettle from the flame, and turn off the gas. Pouring boiling water into a green clay mug, I toss in a peppermint tea bag and flip on the black AM/FM radio sitting on the windowsill. Looking for something worth listening to, the radio hisses, crackles, and hums as I turn the dial. Then, an Ani DiFranco-esque voice and a funky energetic bass line emanate from the small speaker. A woman is singing about food security, animal rights, and pesticides.

What station is this and who is singing? This is not mainstream radio. I am amazed that I can get music like this way out here on Wildhorse Creek Road.

The song ends.

"That was Ember Swift with 'Include My Food' from her 2002 album, *Stiltwalking*. I'm your host, Tom Coxworth and you're listening to Folk Routes on CKUA Radio in Edmonton on this beautiful Saturday afternoon."

Wow! A folk music show in Edmonton? I think to myself. How does this station in Alberta make it all the way to my little cabin on Wildhorse Creek Road in southern British Columbia?

I turn up the volume, walk outside, and stand on the porch, leaving the door open.

Taking a sip of tea, I think about the songs I've written, wondering if I could ever write songs that really matter to people. I wonder what it would be like to be a real musician, one who records albums, tours, sings for audiences, and gets paid to play music.

I walk down the porch steps with my mug and out to the grove of aspens in front of the cabin. Lying on my back at the foot of the trees, I place my mug beside me. My tired, sore body sinks into the soft bed of yellow grass. I look up between the branches and survey the blue afternoon sky above me. Jonah's face appears in my mind, and then, Miles'. Shame simmers in my chest but I take a deep breath and feel the earth, solid, under my body, cradling me. The shame seems to drain from my flesh and down into the ground underneath. Jonah and Miles' faces recede.

I think about being a lesbian.

I wonder if I will ever feel comfortable in this lesbian body.

I wonder what it might be like to live my life with a woman. To come home to a woman, make dinner with her, sit by the fire, and talk with her about the day. To curl my body around her every night and breathe with her as we fall asleep. To love her and feel her love for me. I wonder what it might be like to face my fear and put effort into writing more songs. A lot of songs. To stop letting fear rule over me and start singing my songs in public, in front of people. To take a risk and start living the musical life I had imagined in my mind.

My chest heaves up and down as I sob.

Off in the distance, I hear a dog barking. Two Stellars Jays, perched side by side on the rooftop of the cabin, chit-chat to each other. Towering overhead, like protective, soundless companions, aspen trees stand around me. A warm breeze picks up and their leaves tremble against the blue sky. Breathing in the golden sunshine, my muscles soften into the ground, and I unclench my hands into the grass.

I have to use my fear as fuel. I think to myself. *To propel me forward. This is the only life I've got.*

10
Heal myself[4]
(Reid, 2006)

Sitting here, thinking about my life again
And I don't know if I'll be able to write about anything else
Cuz there's so much about me

And I can feel the Earth moving beneath me
The ants are going about their daily work
And the grass is shifting under my weight
And the weight of my childhood lies heavily on my chest

So, it's time for me to start telling the truth in my life
Stop pretending I don't see or hear anything at all
And I heard a poet quote another poet on some summer's
    day
She said we lie with words and silence, too

Chorus:
Wake me up from this long-lost dream
Cuz I've been sleepwalking for most of my life now
And I don't know if this Earth can be healed
So, I'm working really hard to heal myself

And if you think it's getting better, then let me ask you this:
What if there were no bitch, no whore, no motherfucker
What if it was just fuck you, father?
I said, Fuckyoufather

Chorus:
Wake me up from this long-lost dream
Cuz I've been sleepwalking for most of my life now
And I don't know if this Earth can be healed
So I'm working really hard to heal myself

And what if women weren't afraid
And what if men weren't afraid too
And what if we all stopped to think about our place in this
    world
And what if I could love who I wanted
And what if I could be who I wanted

And I laugh when people tell me they don't want to be extreme
And I say think of this: misogyny's extreme
And patriarchy's extreme and homophobia's extreme
And hatred is extreme and rape is extreme
And unconsciousness is extreme
And consciousness is extreme
And feeling is extreme and freedom is extreme
And choice is extreme and self-love is extreme

By singing, I heal myself
By climbing mountains, I heal myself
By lying under the moon, I heal myself
By telling my stories, I heal myself

Chorus:
Wake me up from this long-lost dream
Cuz I've been sleepwalking for most of my life now
And I don't know if this Earth can be healed
So I'm working really hard to heal myself
I'm working really hard to heal myself

11
Truckdriver[5] (Reid, 2009)

When I was a young girl, I wanted to be a truckdriver
I wanted to drive my whole life away
I would stop at all of the truck stops on the roadside and I'd
Order the special with fries
Then I'd get back in my truck and drive for miles and miles

I grew up on a farm out in southern Ontario, I guess I was a
    lucky girl
But our white picket fence was a bit of a joke, it was broke
    and it fenced me in
Sometimes to get away I would lay myself down
In the sweet summer hay fields at night
I'd watch the headlights on the highway and I would
Dream of a better life

Chorus:
I would drive
I would drive

I got my license when I was seventeen years old, it was my
    freedom ticket

I'd listen to rock 'n' roll on FM radio as I drove those country
    roads
Then I'd pick up a six-pack and a couple of friends and we'd just
Waste time, driving around
I'd feel the wind on my face, then I'd go get drunk in a field
    someplace

Chorus:
I would drive
I would drive

When I was twenty-two, I finished some school, I packed up
    and I
Moved out west
Sitting on my roof above the city smoking hand-rolled
    cigarettes
But there were buildings between me and who I wanted to be
And they started closing in on me
I got that "gotta get me outta this place" feeling again

So, I got me a job stocking shelves for eight bucks an hour in
A small mountain town grocery store
And the women cashiers had been working there for many
    years or more
And their husbands worked the butcher line
While I tried to keep my stock in a straight line
But I was biding time and besides I never was the marrying
    kind

Bridge:
I'm hard because I've had to be

And I'm scarred from my life's accident scenes
But singing taught me to feel something
In the midst of nothing
It got my heart pumping and put my hands on the wheel

Chorus:
I will drive
I will drive

When I was a young girl, I wanted to be a truckdriver

12
The only dyke at the open mic[6] (Reid, 2009)

I was feeling blue the other night
So I walked down the street to the neighbourhood open mic
Thinking if I played a couple of songs
It just might make me feel alright

I walked up to the bar and put down my guitar
And ordered myself a tea because I couldn't afford a beer
And then I sat down and took a look around the place
And surveyed all the faces in there

There were some college kids slamming back a couple
   of pitchers and a
Group of teachers in v-neck sweaters, planning their
   next strike
And on the mic was a Kurt Cobain look-alike in converse
   shoes
Singing some grunge-love, suicide blues

There were some old boys sitting at the bar, giving me
   the stare

They were checking out my hair
And I thought "Oh my god, what am I doing here?
Right now, I could really use that beer."

Chorus:
I'm the only dyke at the open mic
My throat's feeling a little tight and it's getting hot in here
I'm the only dyke at the open mic
I wish I was on that flight tonight, Joni, get me outta here

When Kurt sang his final note
He left the stage to smoke cigarettes and drink himself
    depressed
And the hostess asked if I'd like to play a couple of tunes
Well, I guess I didn't have much to lose

So, I jumped up on stage but I bumped into the mic stand
And it crashed landed to the floor
And the hostess ran up to help me out as I was
Fighting off my second round of self-doubt

Chorus:
I'm the only dyke at the open mic
And the mic's down on the floor and I'm already looking for
    the door
I'm the only dyke at the open mic
I'm just trying to look cool but I'm feeling a bit foolish

Then, it took me what seemed like forever to tune my guitar
And I could hear the old boys at the bar snickering through
    the darkness

And I'm still thinking, "Do I really have to go through
    with this?"

Then the microphone started feeding back on me
And the sound guy freaked out
And I felt like I was in one of those classic movie scenes
You know or like the time when Ellen Degeneres finally came
    out

And the old boys at the bar had their backs to me now
And Kurt Cobain was getting drunk and loud
The teachers were rowdy and ready to call union meeting
    and me?
I was still contemplating leaving

Then, I heard someone say "I hope this chick doesn't stick
    around,
Cuz I've had enough for one day."
And then I ripped into my first song and I blew them
    all away

Chorus:
I'm the only dyke at the open mic
I'm working the crowd and I'm making them laugh out loud
I'm the only dyke at the open mic
Well, what do you know? I was winning 'em over

So, I finished my tunes to a round of whistling and clapping
And I was packing up my guitar case
When one of the old boys from the bar came over
With a really sheepish look on his face

And I'm thinking "OK, what's this guy going to say to me?
I better get ready."
But he slapped me on the shoulder and
He said with a grin, "I loved your songs, man
I wish I was a lesbian."

Chorus:
Yeah, I'm the only dyke at the open mic
Strumming my guitar in this dingy little bar, yeah
I'm the only dyke at the open mic
Belting out songs about women, feeling good when
    I'm singing

Yeah, I'm the only dyke at the open
Strumming my guitar in this dingy little bar
I'm the only dyke at the open mic
Some nights I gotta push myself a little farther

13
In this soul, in this body

Tucked under a large crevice in a mountain, Hedley, British Columbia is a tiny town of approximately 250 people off the Crowsnest Highway which runs along the southern part of British Columbia, near the US border. A craggy, folded orogeny—the result of a geological, metamorphic process where tectonic plates collide followed by intense pressure and deformation of the Earth's crust—looms above the town on the northwest side of the mountain. Opposite the orogeny, balanced on a cliff, are several small, dilapidated wooden structures, remnants of a once-bustling mining operation.

The Hitching Post is the only sit-down restaurant in the town. It looks like something out of a western movie. Glass paned windows make up the storefront, and inside the restaurant, antique farming and mining tools adorn the wood panelled walls: scythes, oxen yokes, garden hoes, shovels of all shapes and sizes, silage knives, pruners, iron post hammers, sickles, rakes, sheep shears, axes, handsaws, pitchforks, flails, chaff cutters, horseshoes.

There's a live music show tonight at the Hitching Post. My tour companions, Sarah, Johanna, and I are performing. Tickets are $30, dinner included—roast chicken or pan-fried brook trout with steamed vegetables, mashed potatoes, and a green garden side salad. A pretty good deal for dinner and some decent live entertainment out in the middle of ranch country.

Sarah, Johanna, and I are singer-songwriters. We each play guitar and sing songs we compose ourselves. Our tour poster describes us as "a rollicking estrogen-injected show of power-house women in folk music from the Canadian West." We are on a six-week tour that will take us all the way from Vancouver British Columbia, where we live, to Ottawa, Ontario. Realizing that being in a city centre would be easier if I wanted to earn a living as a musician, I moved back to Vancouver from the Kootenays three years ago. The Hitching Post in Hedley is the fourth stop on our tour.

After the show, Sarah, Johanna, and I fold up our mic stands, wrap our cables into neatly bound piles, and pack up our guitars. A round, jolly man with round, pink cheeks, a full white beard and moustache approaches me. He has on a red flannel shirt and suspenders, blue jeans, cowboy boots, and a grey felt, cowboy hat.

"Hello Kate, I'm Larry," he says in a raspy voice, tipping his cowboy hat at me.

"Your tunes are great!" he beams. "Thanks for coming all the way to Hedley to sing for us."

"Oh, and," reaching into his shirt pocket, his eyes flashing, he chuckles, "I play harmonica, too!"

He pulls out a little silver harmonica, puts it to his lips, and drones out a cheery, little melody.

Larry has coal worker's pneumoconiosis from working in the mines his whole life. He tells me his voice is hoarse because the coal dust damaged his larynx.

"Yeah, the black lung got me, but I can still play my harp! Hope to see you girls here again!" Larry waves and turns around, his harmonica purring as he hums out another tune and ambles out the door.

Well, what do you know? I think to myself as I continue packing up my gear. Songs like, "Co-op Girlz," "Starving Artist," "The Only Dyke at the Open Mic," and "Everyone's Fucked but Me" narrate my experiences as a lesbian and provide some social commentary on the world I live in. I am amazed that a guy like Larry likes my songs. I smile.

The next morning, I wake up at the Gold Mountain RV Park, a campground east of Hedley. Sarah, Johanna, and I rented a large but modest suite with a kitchenette above the campground office. Drab, partly closed curtains hang from brass curtain rods. Between the worn, light blue fabric, I can see dark green pine trees outside. The heat from the baseboard heater moves in waves as it floats up past the open window. A slice of morning sunlight refracts off the mirror over the sofa bed and spreads across the threadbare, tan-coloured carpet. Sarah and Johanna are curled up on the pull-out sofa bed under a lumpy dark blue and grey comforter. There is a small hole in the corner of the comforter, and cotton stuffing peeks out.

I slide on a pair of shorts and a sweater, some socks and hiking shoes, and a toque. Grabbing a small notebook and pen and stuffing them in my back pocket, I quietly close the door of the rental suite behind me, leaving my tour mates sleeping soundly inside.

Walking down the steps into the crisp morning air, the sweet, pungent smell of Ponderosa pine trees fills my nostrils. Striding up the driveway and across the Crowsnest Highway, I head to the edge of a field. I climb the rusty barbed-wire fence and start ascending the yellow grassy knoll ahead of me, beckoned by a bulky outcrop of rock about 300 metres up ahead.

My heart wakes up from its resting place in my chest, beating faster as my legs carry me up. Yellow, coarse grasses brush against my calves, the incline getting steeper as I climb the hill. My breath quickens as my lungs work harder to take in air. The scent of dry sagebrush and yarrow merges with the scent of the pines.

Arriving at the base of the rock outcrop, I grip the rough, lichened boulders, and scramble to the top of the rocks that jut out over the valley. Morning sunlight slowly spreads across the Crowsnest Highway snaking through the valley below. Mountains treed with pines, rise behind the RV park resting quietly on the other side of the highway. The blue-green ribbon of the Similkameen River weaves in and out of the forest along the valley bottom. Up here, the air is cleaner, my head, clearer and my heart, expansive.

Down at my feet, on a small grassy patch between the rocks lies the femur bone of a deer, clean and bleached white from the sun. I stoop over to inspect it further. The bone is hollow in the middle where the marrow had once been. Thousands of tiny holes punctuate the porous end by the joint, and fine cracks run along the length of the bone. As I reach down and pick it up, a breeze whispers in my ear. Standing up, the bone's weightiness feels good in my hand as I curl my fingers around its solid form.

Without warning, the wind picks up and veils between the worlds blur. The rocky ground beneath me, the RV park, evergreen trees, and mountains across the highway begin to swirl around me, evaporating. Cracking open, I leave my body. Weightless, I am thrown into space as the universe spins around me.

Then, a golden, undulating grassy plain emerges into view, sprawling out before me as far as I can see. Bare feet hitting the ground, I begin to run. The sun streams down my back and my thick, long, chestnut brown hair flows out behind me as I sprint, strong, unencumbered, and wild. The thunderous clamour of pounding hooves fills my ears and clouds of dust billow upwards as a herd of massive animals surrounds me. They charge into my pulsing heart. I am traveling through their bones. Together, we stampede across the sweeping plain stretching out towards the horizon ahead of us.

Then, a jolt of recognition flashes through me: I have been here before. This very place. This very soul. Many lives ago. A different body.

Everything coalesces and comes into sharp focus. The rage, guilt, sorrow, regret, desire, joy, wonder. The traumatic incidents I experienced and witnessed throughout my life that I carry with me. Each person I encountered, came into relationship with, and left. The unhealthy choices I made because I wasn't paying attention. The shame and confusion I felt about myself. The times I wondered how I would find a way home to myself. The question of how to land in a place, and take root, for good. The near-constant ache I feel for the need to express myself and write my version of my story and account for my feelings in song. The sound of my guitar reverberating against my torso and how it feels solid in my arms. The way my body and voice expand when I sing for people on a stage.

My soul has travelled through countless lives, forging for me a path through this world, leading me to this very moment through stories and song. I am at home. In this soul. In this body.

Aware of the firmness of the bone in my hand once again, I release it and it falls to the ground. I drop to my knees. Placing my palms on the ground in front of me, great sobs heave through my chest and out of my mouth. My heart racing, I wail into the morning air, awash in awe and gratitude. Crouching there for a minute, I draw in a deep breath, feeling my lungs expand under my ribs, trying to process what just happened.

Did I imagine this? I pick up the bone, to see if it will happen again. But, it doesn't. Yet, as euphoria swirls inside me, I know I didn't imagine this.

A few yards away, as if laughing at me, two crows chortle and chuckle back and forth from the branch of a lofty Ponderosa pine tree.

"Oh sure!" I yell out to them, wiping the tears from my cheeks, amused.

"Just because you get how all this works, doesn't mean everyone else does, alright?"

Animals. Shaking my head, I chuckle. *They think they know everything.*

Sitting down on the rocky outcrop overlooking the winding highway down below, I pull out my notebook and pen. Language cannot always describe things of the spirit, it seems. But perhaps, sometimes, when paired with music, it comes close.

14
Crying holy[7]
(Reid, 2011)

She came to me in an autumn field
Somewhere west of here
At my feet, she laid a bone down
Old and bleached, on the dusty ground

I picked it up and held it close
Crows singing, Buffalo thunder ringing out
Then, I was running with the herd
Along the great divide between two worlds

Chorus:
I don't know about the whole
But I know tears and bones
And all my broken pieces
And begging for mercy
I'm down on my knees
Crying holy

I had my finger on some kind of trigger
When I was young
I would wake up, wondering how I got there
And how I would make it home

And I never wanted to do what they wanted me to
I just didn't know any other way
And I didn't want to be good
It was just a survival thing

Chorus:
I don't know about the whole
But I know tears and bones
And all my broken pieces
And begging for mercy
I'm down on my knees
Crying holy

I was never meant to
Live in the terrified shadows
Of all the tired and unrealized lives of the
People along my bloodline

And it's good to recognize
All those hard places from where we come
We've got to see beyond the horizon
And look possibility in the eye

When I'm long dead and gone
And all those Crows and those thundering Buffalo
Will come rest on top this place
She'll come back and lay down my bones

Chorus:
I don't know about the whole
But I know tears and bones

And all my broken pieces
And begging for mercy
I'm down on my knees
Crying holy
Crying holy

15
Lesbians and biker dudes

My economy rental car is parked outside a strip mall in south Calgary. My friend, Toni, sits beside me in the passenger seat. It's 2009.

We survey the run-down roadhouse in front of us. A neon Budweiser sign flashes in the large window, just above a large fracture in the glass that's been covered over with clear plastic wrap and duct tape. Cigarette butts litter the sidewalk around a 3-foot, free-standing metal ashtray against the wall. "Legs" by ZZ Top blares through the door, which is propped open with a small, wooden wedge. The words, "Baja Bar and Grill" are painted in large yellow and orange scrawl across the cracked window, flanked by a couple of hand-painted, faded green palm trees. Toni and I look at each other and then back at the shabby tavern before us. We are silent.

Like me, Toni is a singer-songwriter. She's got a local fan base in Calgary and we're doing a couple of gigs together in Alberta. Tonight, we were scheduled to play at Money Pennies, the local dyke drinkery in Calgary. But, a day before our show, Calgary city hall closed Money Pennies down indefinitely. Some kind of health and safety infraction, we heard.

Toni and I scramble to move our show to another venue. The Baja is the only bar in town that will take a last-minute live music booking.

Staring at the row of gleaming Harley Davidson and Yamaha motorbikes lined up, side by side in front of our car, I exhale loudly.

"I don't know, Tone. I'm feeling a bit sketchy about this. It doesn't look like the kind of place where they're going to be into having a couple of queers singing on stage."

"Pfffft. Yeah." Toni sighs.

"But," she pauses, "a few people told me they were coming tonight so hopefully that will help?"

She doesn't sound convinced. Tiny butterflies swirl in the pit of my stomach.

A couple of women in snug, low-cut t-shirts, tight jeans, and high heels stumble out of the bar and onto the sidewalk. They each light up a cigarette, dissolving onto each other's shoulders in raucous laughter. Then, a beer-bellied man in a black Rolling Stones t-shirt, Levi's, and cowboy boots staggers outside to join them.

"Heyyyy laaaaadies!" he drones as he fishes a lighter out of the pocket of his jeans.

"Can I join you?" Not waiting for them to answer, he lights up. Taking a puff of his cigarette, he leans up against the glass storefront of the roadhouse. He runs a hand along his receding hairline and down his long grey, ponytailed hair.

Toni and I look at each other again, roll our eyes, and groan. I wonder if we might run into trouble tonight.

"Well, this should be interesting. We can't turn back now," I say, checking my watch. "Should we get at it, buddy? It's 7 p.m. and we're on at 8."

"Yep. Let's do it," Toni replies. We hoist ourselves out of the car, walk around to the trunk and pop it open.

I grab my guitar and a carry-on suitcase that has my gear in it: patch cables, XLR cables, a microphone, harmonicas and two harmonica holders, a tuning pedal, a DI box, extra guitar straps, a guitar stand, a binder with lyric sheets, a music stand, and CDs to sell. Toni heaves her guitar and a leather satchel with her gear out of the trunk. Slamming the trunk closed, we walk to the door of the bar.

"Howdy, ladies," the man drawls.

"Hey," I give a cheery nod. "How's it going?"

I know this kind of guy, I think to myself. *Thinks he's God's gift to women. But, oblivious. And, harmless.*

"Better now that you two are here, honey," he grins as smoke seeps out from between his lips.

"Ok," I say, rolling my eyes. Toni and I slip past them and walk inside.

I hear one of the women outside laughing, "Oh my God, Steve! Don't be such a player."

Inside, the reek of spilled beer permeates the air. I catch the familiar whiff of stale cigarettes. Thankfully, there's a law against smoking inside bars now.

As my eyes adjust to the dim light, I see a group of men—black leather vests, t-shirts, long hair, tanned tattooed forearms, faded blue jeans, cowboy boots, a couple of them wearing sunglasses—standing at the bar, yakking and barking around pints of lager. Three tight-panted, made-up women with cream-coloured skin are sitting at one of the tables. One has a fluffy spiral perm of long chestnut-coloured hair. Another has platinum bleach-blonde hair pulled back in a high ponytail that swings while she talks. The other one has shoulder-length, dyed auburn hair with dark brown roots, and feathery, hair-sprayed bangs. I used to have hair like that when I was a teenager. *The '80s called*, I chuckle to myself. *It wants its hairstyles back.*

The women chatter and snicker, sipping cocktails from tall slim glasses. They look over at the men at the bar. One of them fiddles with the straw in her glass as she whispers to the others. They cackle some more and slurp their drinks.

Squinting past them, I catch a glimpse of myself in a mirror that's hanging up behind the bar. I feel a sudden combination of awkwardness and confidence as I inspect the person before me: a bright, red faux-hawk, red- and black-striped tie, and a black button-down with rolled-up sleeves. I feel out of place, but I like the way I look. Sometimes feeling out of place feels good.

As Toni and I run through our sound check, a few groups of women walk into the bar and sit down at a few tables near the back. Talking and laughing, a couple of them order drinks. They look up and wave to Toni. Toni waves back.

"You were right," I grin at Toni. "The lesbians showed up. Awesome."

"Yeah, man!" Toni gives me a thumbs-up as she adjusts her guitar strap and places her set list down on the floor in front of her.

As I exhale and my shoulders loosen, I feel a sense of relief. At least some of the people in this place will appreciate our songs. I bend the mic stand towards my mouth, plug in my guitar, and start tuning it.

After sound check, Toni and I introduce ourselves to the people in the audience and thank everyone for coming. The audience cheers and some of the lesbians raise their drinks.

"Hell yeah!" one of them yells. "A Toni Vere and Kate Reid show? Anytime!" The other lesbians cheer and take swigs from their glasses.

Then, Toni launches into one of her best-loved songs, "My G-String." The lesbians hoot and holler as they jump up from their tables. Waving their hands in the air, they weave up to the front and out onto the scuffed wooden dance floor in front of the stage. They dance and clap and laugh and sing along with Toni, shaking their hips.

The biker dudes look at one another, raising their eyebrows. Smirking, they put down their beers and saunter towards the crowd of lesbians on the dance floor. Weaving in and out of the gyrating bodies, the bikers beam at each other. They stomp their cowboy boots and wobble their hips, bumping up against the lesbians. The lesbians look at one another and guffaw, twirling and swaying around the dance floor. One of the lesbians grabs one of the bikers and dances the two-step with him. He looks at his buddies and winks. They spur him on.

When Toni finishes singing, I break into "Doing It for the Chicks." The lesbians shriek, shimmying up against one another. With their thumbs hooked in the belt loops of their Levi's, the bikers jig and kick up their boots. The lesbians bump and grind with the bikers, and the bikers bump and grind with the lesbians. Pitching over with laughter, the lesbians whirl and cavort around one another, howling.

Then, I hit the chorus.

> *I'm just doing it for the chicks*
> *I'm just singing hoping to make it with you, baby*
> *All I need is my god-given ability to serenade*
> *And I'm on a full-blown recruiting crusade*
> *I've got me a pocket rhyming dictionary*
> *I got me a couple of killer hot licks*
> *But the music's all just extracurricular*
> *Cuz' I'm just doing it for the chicks*

Suddenly, the colour drains from the faces of the biker dudes. Like light bulbs go on, one by one, in their heads. They all stop dancing and look at one another. As I strum exuberantly on my guitar and wail on my harmonica, they rotate around, as if executing a well-rehearsed choreographed dance move, and slink quietly to the back of the bar together. Shoulders slumped, they hunker over their beers.

When I finish my song, I hoot, "And all the guys just figured out what's going on!"

The lesbians on the dance floor break out in boisterous laughter, clapping and screeching. Toni and I join in. I glance at the biker dudes. They have sheepish grins on their faces.

After that, I'm not so worried about our safety. The biker dudes are just a bunch of harmless old boys out looking for a good time.

As Toni sings her next song, I ponder what just happened. Perhaps the biker dudes learned something. Perhaps they realized that they're not always the centre of attention in every room they stroll into. That not all women need men around to have a good time. That lesbians exist and congregate in unexpected public spaces.

And perhaps Toni, and the lesbians, and I learned something too. Perhaps we realized that we can find each other—even in run-down drinking dives full of bikers. That there is something to the phrase "strength in numbers." That it's exhilarating being "the majority" now and then, even when our fears about being targeted still lurk in the backs of our minds.

And me? I will always remember the night Toni Vere and I sang to the lesbians and the biker dudes at the Baja Bar and Grill in south Calgary.

16
Uncle Jim

I am jammed in between two people on the 99 B-Line bus in Vancouver. Every seat is filled and bodies are squeezed shoulder to shoulder along the entire aisle. Like an enormous can of sardines on wheels, the bus lurches along Broadway Avenue en route to the campus of The University of British Columbia, where I am doing my master's degree. Grabbing the edge of the window behind me, I slide it open. The fresh saltwater air of English Bay floats into the bus and blows across my face. Warm autumn afternoon sun streams in through the window. It's 2013.

I look around me. Mostly students. Earbuds in. Heads down. Thumbs scrolling or swiftly tapping out text messages on their phones. Pulling out my phone, I notice an email from my sister, Ava. The subject heading says, "Be prepared."

My lungs constrict. I know it's about our Uncle Jim, our's mother's eldest brother. He was admitted to Sunnybrook Hospital in Toronto a few days ago. Our mom has been visiting him every day since he was admitted. Ava went to visit him yesterday. Jim is 75 years old, and he is dying.

I take a deep breath and open Ava's email. There are three photos. Jim is stretched out in a hospital bed, his head and torso slightly propped up by pillows. His slight frame is draped in a thin, light blue hospital sheet and a worn, beige blanket. His face is grey and gaunt, like the life is slowly seeping out of him. Silver stubble covers his cheeks and chin. His once straight dark brown hair is salt-and-pepper grey and thinning. Our mom is beside his bed.

In one photo, she leans over the stainless-steel bedside railing with her hand on his arm, as if she's consoling him.

In another, their hands are clasped in the air above his body, as if she's trying to restrain him and he is resisting, his face grimacing.

In another, his eyes are closed, and our mom sits in a chair beside his bed. Her hand rests on his shin.

I read Ava's email. She tells me that Jim is delirious, and that he doesn't know what's happening or why he's in the hospital. She tells me that she was there visiting him yesterday and that she and Mom are going back to see him today.

Sorrow floods my heart. Flipping my phone over, I shift my body to peer out the window. One by one, tall feathery green cedar trees and large white and grey stucco houses whizz by. In between them, I catch glimpses of English Bay and the mountains across the water—Capilano Mountain, Grouse Mountain, and Mount Seymour—pointing into the blue sky.

I don't know Jim well, but growing up, I always liked him. When I was a child, I saw him a handful of times a year. When I moved away from home as an adult, I would only see him if he was at the farm, visiting my mom, when I flew back from British Columbia to see my family.

Jim is not like my other uncles. My whole life, he never had a girlfriend and never married. He was soft-spoken and gentle.

Mysterious and private. Quirky and peculiar. He worked as a travel agent and lived alone in a one-bedroom apartment off Yonge Street, one of the busiest streets in Toronto. Living in the city, he didn't need a driver's license. He walked or took the subway or streetcar to get around.

Resembling my grandmother, Nana, more than he did Poppy, my grandfather, Jim was slender, unimposing. When he smoked, a Matinee Slim extra mild rested between long, thin fingers— fingers that looked like Nana's, except more delicate, and without the polish. Cigarette smoke curled around his slight frame when he talked in a soft, nasal voice. Broody, but in a pleasant, gentle kind of way, he complained a lot. Perhaps this is why I liked him. He was down to earth in a way that my other family members are not.

A couple of times, when Ava and I were young adults—before I began to realize I was queer—we pondered whether Jim might be gay. But, he never disclosed anything, and we never asked him. We didn't know him well enough to ask a question like that.

Besides, we weren't that kind of family. The kind of family that talked about personal things or had gay people in it. We were a white, middle-class family who appeared as normal as possible. At family gatherings, my father occasionally performed his impression of an effeminate gay man while my Uncle Jack and Uncle Seth, Jim's brothers, laughed. Lesbians were never mentioned. And, transgender people? Forget it.

My phone buzzes on my lap. I flip it over. Tapping the green "accept" button, I put the phone to my ear. People standing in the aisle pitch sideways, as the bus roils and sways around a corner.

"Hi, Mom." I say, quietly, not wanting to disturb the people around me on the bus. "Poor Jimmy. How are *you*?"

"It's hard seeing Jim this way. The dementia is bad. He's really confused and gets upset easily. He's so thin and he's hardly eating," her voice cracks. "Ava and I are going to visit him in a bit."

She tells me that, over the years, she tried to talk with Jim about his identity. She never directly asked him if he was gay but, she dropped hints now and then. She had hoped that he would trust her enough to confide in her and come out of the closet. That he would stop being so secretive and open up to her about his life. But, he never did.

"Sometimes, I used to call him on the phone just to catch up in the evenings, you know, to find out how he was doing," she reveals.

"But, there were some nights when he didn't answer the phone. So, I would leave a message on his answering machine. Then, he would call back the next day and tell me that he was out walking the night before. I always told him I didn't think it was safe for him to be doing that. It worried me, you know? He went walking alone at night a lot in Toronto. How would he defend himself if something bad happened? He was so gentle and unimposing."

"Yeah, that would worry me, too, Mom," I said.

"So, this morning, I called his friend, David, to let him know that Jim is dying."

"Who's David?" I ask.

"David's been a friend of Jim's for a long time. I met him a couple of times in Toronto when Jim and I had lunch. Years ago, Jim had given him my number and Nana and Poppy's too. David was the one who called me when Jim first started to show signs of being ill. When Jack and I moved Jim from his apartment into assisted living before he went to Sunnybrook, David helped. He's a really nice man."

"Oh." I respond. I had never heard of David before.

"Anyway, I wanted to give David an update on Jim's health. I told him about the phone calls at night and Jim not answering the phone some nights and how he would tell me that he was out walking at night and how I would worry about him. Then, David said, 'Elizabeth, Jim wasn't out walking on those nights when he didn't answer his phone. He was out at the clubs on Church Street, meeting men.'"

Stunned, I suck in my breath. Church Street was the main street in the gay village in Toronto.

"David told me that Jim did that a lot. Picking up men he didn't know and sleeping with them. Even right up until the time he was admitted to Sunnybrook," she added. "David calls it, 'cruising.'"

"Yeah, Mom," I confirm. "That's what it's called."

We talk for a couple more minutes. She says the hardest thing about it all was that she never really got to know her own brother. And, that he never really got to know her.

Blinking back tears, I dab the corners of my eyes with my sleeve.

"I'm so sorry, Mom."

I tell her I will call her again later today on my way home from school. We say goodbye and hang up. I exhale through pursed lips.

My phone buzzes again. It's Ava. I pick it up.

"Hi. How are you doing?" I ask.

Ava describes what's been happening at the hospital and how Jim is doing—sometimes lucid and chatty, sometimes dazed and incoherent. She tells me that she and Mom don't ask him any questions about his life, and he doesn't offer anything. What matters, she says, is being in the moment with him and caring for him as his body rapidly declines.

"Yeah, that makes sense," I reply.

"It must have taken him so much energy to hide himself from us all these years," she muses.

"Totally," I agree.

My heart feels like it's being squeezed. I think about the things I have done over the years to hide my identity from people. I wonder what kinds of things Jim did to keep his a secret.

Thanking Ava for being there for Jim and for Mom, I feel a twinge of guilt about living so far away from my family. But, I am used to that feeling.

We say goodbye and hang up.

My throat tightens. It's hard to accept that Jim, the gay uncle I never really had a chance to know, is dying, helpless, in a hospital bed, thousands of kilometers away. It's hard to accept that even on his deathbed, he still can't bring himself to reveal who he is.

The heaviness of grief and loss spreads across my chest. Grief and loss for Jim's life, shrouded in secrecy. That he was unable to have full, honest relationships with his family members. That I was cheated out of the joy of a connection with a gay elder to whom I could look for advice and talk about "gay things" and what it meant to live and love differently from what surrounded us in rural, southern Ontario. That, among our family, Jim and I never experienced feeling that we weren't alone in our queerness. That homophobia can wrap its insidious grip around us, like tentacles, thick and coarse, trying to strangle the life from our queer bodies.

As the bus hurtles towards campus, I stare out the window. Giant coniferous trees of the Pacific West Coast rush by and I weep silently, praying no one notices.

17
I whispered
the word, "lesbian"

A dear (straight cis) friend is visiting me at my bachelor
    apartment
at the corner of 1st and Balsam in Kitsilano and
she asks about what my master's thesis is about.

I tell her about my research
and how I have been theorizing
how we can construct lineages through other means rather
    than simply
through bloodlines and families of origin and heterosexual
    relationships but
that we can create lineages and kinship lines through artistic
    practices
like songwriting and singing and performance in public
    spaces and
that songs come from bodies and merge with other bodies,
    joining us in music.

I talked about what it was like growing up in the absence of
queer family role models and elders—any role models or
    elders, actually—

who could teach me, show me, reassure me, empower me
with the knowledge that there is
a different way of living,
a different way of loving.

Then,
after all these years
of being out,
after all these years of
thinking about it and reading about it and talking about it
and singing about it and writing about it and living it
I whisper the word "lesbian."

I whisper the word, "lesbian"
so her daughter wouldn't hear it
so my dear (straight cis) friend wouldn't feel uncomfortable,
    awkward, worried
in case her daughter asks what it means
and my dear (straight cis) friend has to explain what it means
to be lesbian, a woman who loves another woman, who
    makes a life with a woman.

I whisper the word, "lesbian"
so I wouldn't feel uncomfortable, awkward, worried
about saying it too loudly, too boldly
for fear of being accused of broadcasting my sexuality and
    flaunting my sexual desire
(because you know, straight people *never* flaunt theirs in
    public)
for being too feminist
for being a man-hater.

After all these years, what is this shame, this internalized
    homophobia
that lives quietly inside me and uncoils stealthily
rising up from the depths of my body
and into my thoughts at unexpected moments
poisoning my heart, my mind, and my relationships with its
    venom?

Why must I try to protect
my dear (straight cis) friend and
her daughter and
myself from
my truth
this truth
this beauty
this joy
this pride
my power?

That day, I whispered the word "lesbian."
Now, I am going to shout it out loud:

I AM A LESBIAN!

I AM A LESBIAN!

I AM A LESBIAN.

18
Rape fantasy

Content warning: This story contains details of violence.

It's not like I'm trying to protect you or anything
if I could remember your name
I would write it in BIG CAPITAL LETTERS ALL OVER THIS PAGE
a million times
for everyone to see.
then, I would flick a lighter, hold it to the page and
burn it

then, I would look you up
come and find you
sometime in the dead
of winter
in Banff

I'd track you down when you're shopping for your groceries
    at the local Safeway
I'd find you in the meat section
flirt with you shamelessly
surrounded by hunks of
freshly cut red flesh
not red like
the colour

of paper hallmark card valentines
in the stores
in early February but
dark red
the colour of
my pumping heart and the
boiling rivers in my veins
the colour of
my seething rage

I'd flirt with you some more
then ask you
out for dinner
go somewhere romantic
be really nice
sweet
smiling
tilt my head to the side
listening
nodding
asking you questions about your life
like I'm
interested
in you
as a person

and when dinner is over
entice you with coy looks
from under my lashes
pouty lips smiling

I'd lure you into my pick-up truck (the one with the
    bumper stickers that reads: real women drive trucks, my
    other car is a broom, well-behaved women rarely make
    history)

let's go parking, I'd say
drive to the Bow River somewhere outside the city limits
somewhere where it's dark
park the truck in a secluded spot
move towards you
pretend to be all hot and bothered
breathing heavy
get all kinky and shit
take off my underwear and
stuff it between your teeth
tie a bandana around your mouth
tie up your hands
behind your back
really tight

that's a bit too tight you smirk through the cloth
thinking that you're gonna get laid

shutthefuckup, I'd say
and tie it tighter
pull out a gun
point it at your face
your eyes bulging wide-open, whites showing
who'ssmirkingnowmotherfucker?
remembermenowmotherfucker?

get the fuck out of my truck, I'd say
start walking, I'd say

I'd follow you, gun at your head
push you to the edge of the frigid current
of the Bow River
your muted begging through
the bandana and my underwear in your mouth
satisfying me

I'd tell you again
startwalkingmotherfucker
into the swirling ice blue water
up to your knees
up to your thighs
up to your
pieceofshitdick
shrinking
in the icy currrent
crying
fucking
freezing
endless
fucking

howmanymoreweretherebesidesmemotherfucker?

I'd consider squeezing
my forefinger and thumb together

I'd consider
what would be better

you dying here in these glacial waters,
your corpse carried away by the current
washing up on the shore down near Calgary
your body a buffet for coyotes
your eyes pecked out by ravens

or

you living and
dragging yourself out of the roiling waters
walking down the highway back to town after dark
trying to explain
to someone who drives by and picks you up why
your jeans are wet, stiff and frozen
your hands are tied behind your back
your mouth is gagged with some woman's underwear

then waking up in the middle of the night
sweatsoaked
nightmares of all the angry women you raped over the years
nightmares of staring down the barrel of a gun
trying to forget
Can't forget
won't forget
I won't forget

so
I'd let you live
live with it
live with this

I'd leave you there
in the frigid pitch black Banff winter and

walk
slowly
back
to
my truck (oh yeah, the other bumpersticker says: coexist)

get in

and

drive

the

fuck

away.

19
When I was a little boy[8] (Reid, 2011)

I met a little boy in my dreams one night
He was living in the trees, that was his home
He slept alone in an old wooden box
No-one to hold him tight, frightened as he was

In bare feet, he was walking on broken glass
He used some shards to cut a way to his lonely heart
His clothes were torn, hair in a tattered mess
There was despair hanging in that forest air

Chorus:
Oh, I was a little boy
When I was a little girl
It was a fine line for me back then
Oh, I was a wild child
When I was a boy

I grew into a tough girl anyway
I knew the summer sun would come and save me from it all
And, I could run around outside in my underwear
I didn't wear a shirt; I had nothing to hide back then

I styled my Barbie's hair with a pair of kitchen scissors
And a rebellious tomboy fantasy
I'd play the husband or the hero
In every single make-believe scene

Chorus:
Oh, I was a little boy
When I was a little girl
It was a fine line for me back then
Oh, I was a wild child
When I was a boy

Bridge:
They say you can be whoever you want to be
With some restrictions on that, you see
Boys should be boys and girls should be girls
The world doesn't sit well with anyone in between
When I was young, I was the son my father never had
And the daughter who tried to make up for that
Now that I'm older, I am the woman I want to be
With a little bit of boy living on in me

Chorus:
Oh, I was a little boy
When I was a little girl
It was a fine line for me back then
Oh, I was a wild child
When I was a boy

20
A story of leaving

I stand at the sandy edge of the Pacific Ocean one last time
looking across Burrard Inlet at the peaks of the north shore
    mountains
as briny ripples of water and bits of seaweed swirl around my
    bare feet.
My heart splits open at the seams
a torrent of sorrow floods out of my ribcage and spills out
    onto the sand and
is carried out to sea.

British Columbia,
land of my second birth—my queer birth—
How can I leave you?
How do I say goodbye?
How can you let me go?

British Columbia,
your land coaxed me to unearth
a different person cowering inside of me
the land that invited me to imagine my queer self
allowed me let go of
who I was
and step into

who I was becoming
who I might be able to be
who I was yearning to be.

British Columbia, you threw me a lifeline and rescued
    me from
the grip of life-long shame
and gave me a place where I could
settle into my body for the first time.
You taught me
how to love a woman
how to love myself
how to love the world.

You gifted me the revelation that came with
waking up beside a woman's body for the first time
my body pressed up against the softness of hers
the outline of her hips that traced the curve of the
    mountain ridge
that stood outside the window of the bedroom I rented
in a mobile home in Pass Creek on the outskirts of that
    small, pulp-mill town.

Then, those log cabin nights by candlelight
snowflakes falling softly through the open window,
landing on my eyelashes and
the creamy and naked skin of her body,
a land of unexplored meadows and valleys
as a full, white moon rose up
from between the mountains into the indigo sky.

British Columbia,
I am forever grateful for you—
your lands welcomed me
your skies mirrored me
your mountains called out to me
your forests embraced me
your rivers flowed through me
your wild winds purified me
your animals guided me
your soils healed me.

British Columbia,
the music I composed with you is embedded in my soul,
these songs ring out in my heart,
these lyrics are inscribed across the insides of my body.

British Columbia,
I will always love you.

British Columbia,
good-bye.

21
Her

My plane touches down on the runway and
I can't wait to disembark.

Because, her.

Lori is waiting for me at the bustling
Pearson International Airport in Toronto, Ontario, and
I can't wait to press my face into the soft skin scent of her
    neck and
breathe in that men's cologne she wears, the scent of
    coconuts and spice.

The doors of the baggage claim swing open and
I hoist my luggage off the conveyor belt and rush towards
    the exit
Striding out into the large open area of the arrivals gate
I search for her in the sea of waiting people

There she is craning her neck as she
searches for me in the crowd of passengers
I hurry down the ramp, weaving in and out and all around of
the people in front of me walking
so i-n-c-r-e-d-i-b-l-y s-l-o-w-l-y

Please get out of my way! I plead silently in my head
Don't you people know that the love of my life is waiting for me?

*Don't you know that, in grade eleven, I sat beside this woman in
    science class?*
*Don't you know that she and I reunited 25 years later by
    accident—fate likely—at a gig I was playing in Guelph,
    Ontario?*

All the while I'm trying to compose myself—
to hide the fact that I have been weeping for the last 20
    minutes of the flight
as the plane descended over the patchwork Ontario
    landscape of my childhood
those checkerboard fields, hues of brown and green,
so familiar to my eyes, my body, my feet—
and the feel of the moist ground between my toes
    when I used to
kick off my shoes and walk along the dark furrowed rows of
freshly-tilled, spring soil on our farm
a life I left many years ago
a life that is now reviving itself
a life to which I am now returning but reincarnated into
    a body queer.

And suddenly, our eyes meet, and Lori recognizes me
She knows I've been crying, and she's been crying too
and my heart tries to jump out of my chest.
And when the crowd in front of me finally disperses
And she stands before me, a homecoming, familiar
    and tender

I fall against her body into her quiet strength, overcome.
It all comes rushing in—
that everything in my life has led me
back to her, to this moment, to this continuation of our story
to this Ontario soil.

This coming home is something of the heart, the body,
    the spirit
This coming home to her
to these old farm fields
to myself again
to a land I left behind—
how it all falls together
how it all collects in the soft places
inside me.

22
Something 'bout you and me[9] (Reid, 2016)

It all started back in '87
We were seventeen sitting side by side in science class
And instead of paying attention to what the teacher had to say
I made it my personal mission to make you laugh

You were brainy, and I was always getting in trouble
Because studying biology wasn't really my thing
All that talk about cells and genes didn't do it for me
But I learned something about chemistry

Chorus:
I felt Newton's law of attraction with your body next to mine
I was more of a hands-on learner anyway
And Plato's law of affinity flashed across my mind
I guess those old boys knew something 'bout you and me

I was dating a boy and teaching myself to play guitar
You were playing sports and doing your homework

And you passed that class because you were good at science
    and math
And I failed miserably but I never forgot your laugh

And then twenty-five years later, I was playing music on the road
And I ran into you in bar in Ontario
We didn't recognize each other 'til you put two and two
    together
Your math skills came in handy that day

Chorus:
I felt Newton's law of attraction with your body next to mine
I'm more of a hands-on learner anyway
And Plato's law of affinity flashed across my mind
I guess those old boys knew something 'bout you and me

I want to study the curves of your anatomy
Forget what I've learned about love and begin again
Traverse your skin, discovering the wonder that's within
Revere the mystery that brought us here again

Chorus:
I feel Newton's law of attraction when your body's next to
    mine
I'm kind of a hands-on learner anyway
And Plato's law of affinity flashes across my mind
I guess those old boys knew something 'bout you and me

23
Somewhere in between

As I think back to a few years ago, I remember what tipped me off.

I was sitting at my desk in my small, west-facing eighth floor bachelor apartment in Kitsilano, a neighbourhood in Vancouver. Sunlight sparkled on the ocean water of English Bay and in the distance, the dark outline of Vancouver Island merged into the light blue sky. It was 2014 and I was working on my master's thesis.

My cell phone jingled, notifying me of an incoming text message. I picked it up and read a message from a young trans friend in Calgary.

Chase announced to me that he had just undergone top surgery—the gender-affirming surgical removal of breast tissue coupled with the contouring of the remaining chest tissue to build a masculine chest. No sooner did I read his text message than a photo of his naked, newly flat, scarred, sculpted chest popped up in front of me, followed by a string of exclamation marks.

Anger jolted through me like an electric current, evaporating a split second later.

Of course, I didn't share that startling response with him—I knew better than that. Chase was in his early twenties back then and so proud of his new chest. He was ecstatic and I felt honoured that he shared that exciting part of his transition with me. I whooped and hollered in text-speak. I send him a flurry of emojis. Then, I called him to congratulate him.

Once we were done talking, and I put my phone down, question after question bubbled up inside of me.

> *How come Chase can send a photo of his naked chest to me, and it's not perceived as something private or sexual? How come he gets to be free of wearing a bra ever again? How come he now gets to look good in men's dress shirts and I have to get mine tailored to fit my curvy frame because I can't find a store that makes clothes for queer women like me? How come he gets to put his hand on his chest and rub it in public, like some guys do when they're talking or thinking, but if I did that, people would think I was getting fresh with myself? How come he gets to walk around with a flat chest, without all the sexualized meaning of breasts while I have to bear the weight of that meaning every minute of every day? How come I have to carry these cumbersome mounds of flesh around with me—mounds of flesh that feel like they belong to everyone else but me, like all the people I've ever dated, strangers on the street, and even people I've never even met?*

I remember my stomach churning and my heart pounding. I couldn't focus on my thesis. I needed some fresh air. I got up from my desk, pulled on my shoes, and walked out the door of my apartment.

Two blocks from my apartment, I picked my way through the barnacle-covered rocks scattered along the beach. The sun warmed my face as I breathed in the salty air. The mountains of West and North Vancouver stood like silent guardians off in the distance. An eagle circled above, keeping an eye on me. Eagles always seemed to show up when I needed them to.

It didn't take me long to realize that the jolt of anger I felt when I saw Chase's naked chest was disguised jealousy.

"Shit," I muttered under my breath.

I wanted a chest like that. I craved the kind of bodily freedom my young trans friend now gets to experience. I yearned for a say in how I felt inside my body and how people read me on the outside.

The problem is, I didn't identify as transgender. I stopped walking and sat down on a large boulder on the beach.

When I began to learn about feminism and encountered feminist women in my early twenties, I aligned with the label, "woman," and for many years, I identified that way. Using the word "woman" rather than "lady" or "girl" gave me a sense of strength, a sense of pride. "Woman" felt powerful and allowed me to rise above the sexist, misogynistic language, stories, and jokes that engulfed me as a young person. "Woman" became a badge of resistance and a symbol of survival.

Then, over the years, I became exposed to other ways of under-standing and defining gender. I began to think more expan-sively about all the discursive constraints and norms that society imposes on people's bodies. I began to question my own gender identity and how I feel about my body. I encountered the term "cisgender." But, like the term, "trans," I didn't use "cisgender" to describe myself either. It didn't feel accurate, and I feltl irritated that there seemed to be a new expectation to use the word in certain circles if one didn't identify as trans.

I remember thinking, *But, if I don't identify as cis or trans, then what labels do I use? What if I want top surgery? Where do I fit?*

At the time, I didn't know anyone else like me—in my mid-forties, who identified—reluctantly—as a woman but didn't want breasts. All the people I knew who were having top surgery identified as trans men. Like Chase, they were young, decades younger than I am. They took testosterone, used he/him or they/them pronouns, and changed their names to reflect their masculinity.

I was doing none of those things. Sure, I was gender non-conforming, but, back then, I still used she/her pronouns. I bore the name my parents gifted me at birth, the name of my great maternal grandmother: Katharine (Kate, as everyone knew me). Aside from my breasts, I felt mostly fine with the rest of my anatomically female body.

I arrived back at my apartment building and rode the elevator back up to the eighth floor. Sitting back down at my desk, I returned to my master's thesis.

A couple of weeks later, I rode my bike over to East Vancouver to see my doctor for my annual physical check-up. At the end of the appointment, I decided to take a chance. I told her I had a question.

"Go ahead," she smiled, expenctantly.

I swallowed. My palms felt clammy.

"I am starting to realize that I don't like having breasts," I murmured, looking at my hands in my lap. "I'm wondering about top surgery."

My doctor stiffened. The air in the room changed.

"I don't know anything about that, sorry," she replied.

"It's okay," I said quickly, jumping off the examination table. As red flush crept up my neck, I thank her and left, scurrying out of her office, down the steps, and onto Commercial Drive towards my locked-up bike.

Maybe it's just not possible. Maybe I'm just being absurd, I thought as I cycled home.

****

A few years later during the spring of 2018, I am walking down the hallway at the University of Toronto with a classmate of mine during a graduate student conference.

Rae and I are doctoral students, both interested in research about gender and sexuality. As we walk, we talk about bodies and identity and gender, when suddenly, I blurt out, "I don't identify as trans, but I wish I could have top surgery."

Rae stops me, puts their hand on my shoulder, and looks me in the eyes.

"You *can* have top surgery. It's *your* body," they declare. "The gender train makes *all* the stops into the station."

Rae didn't ask intrusive questions or suggest that I should learn how to be comfortable with the body I was born into. They explain that, in Ontario, people no longer have to identify as transgender or be working towards a medical or legal gender transition to qualify for healthcare coverage for gender-affirming surgeries. They tell me that gender non-conforming, non-binary, and genderqueer people can access this surgery and that top surgery is covered by our provincially funded medical plan. They suggest that I talk with my doctor about it and see about getting a referral to a surgeon.

Rae's message is, simply, "you can do this."

A lightning bolt of joy shoots through me.

I feel like I have been given a gift. To change my body so that it lines up with how I feel inside—even though I am struggling to define a gender I still can't name? Rae just opened a door for me and welcomed me into a new world, into a spacious dwelling of possibility.

Tears prickle in my eyes and spill down my cheeks. I can't find words to speak. I excuse myself, slipping into a nearby washroom to compose myself.

The next day, I call the University of Toronto Health and Wellness Centre and make an appointment with my doctor.

At my appointment, I talk with my doctor about what I've been going through. That I have been struggling with my body for a long time. That I cannot live with my breasts any longer.

"Okay! Tell me more." she responds.

I explain how I've been feeling about my body for several years. How my understanding of my gender has been shifting. How my feelings towards my body have also been shifting. I announce that I would like to get top surgery, and I ask for her help.

Asking me a few more questions, she is kind and supportive when I respond. She tells me what steps we need to take so that I can get top surgery. The process is straightforward. The conversation with her is easy. We do some paperwork.

This time, I have the words. This time, my doctor listens.

Thanking her, I leave her office and go outside. Awash in gratitude and disbelief, I sit down on the curb of St. George Street, sobbing.

****

In the months, weeks, and days leading up to my surgery date, questions and fears plague me, punctuating my mind with increasingly rapid fire:

> *Who am I going to tell about this surgery? And how? And why?*
>
> *What if after my breasts are gone, I decide I want to take testosterone and identify as a man?*
>
> *What if my cis-women friends think of this as an act of betrayal of all things feminine?*
>
> *What if my partner thinks my scarred, flat chest is ugly and I have to keep my shirt on when we are being intimate?*
>
> *What if, one day, while I'm walking down Bloor Street in Toronto, my body suddenly splits open at the incision site and my insides spill out all over the sidewalk in front of people?*
>
> *What if I accidentally die on the operating table?*

A few months later, on November 8, 2018, at the age of 47, I undergo top surgery.

After surgery, all my questions and fears evaporate. Top surgery makes me feel at home in my skin. It gives me the sense of being at ease in my clothes. My body finally feels like it belongs to me and is made up of the parts *I* want. I relish being in-between.

I begin using the label "genderqueer" to describe myself. Some people use the label, "non-binary" to describe their gender, but that word doesn't fit for me. I have worked so hard in my life to become someone, I don't want to be "non" anything. To me, genderqueer is not connected to the binary in any way. To me, "genderqueer" feels expansive, disruptive, and open to possibility. Genderqueer feels queer.

Four years later, I change my name to Kael. I begin using they/them pronouns.

Several years after having top surgery, I am still astonished every time I look in the mirror. I am grateful that I listened to the wisdom—others' and my own—that led me to this decision. I am thankful for the people in my life who cheered me on and supported me through the process of top surgery, and for those who congratulated me after it was done.

Sometimes, when I'm in public, I put my hand to my chest and marvel at its flat, streamlined shape.

Finally, I am grounded and thriving somewhere in between.

*   This chapter is dedicated to Dr. Sue Harrison and Dr. Melinda Musgrave.

24
Together

I wake up to the June sun streaming in the east-facing
    balcony door
of my one room apartment on St. George Street in Toronto
cardinals chirping together outside on the leafy branches of
    an old oak tree
bedcovers thrown off my double bed, clothes strewn across
    the tile floor
me, shirtless, my Fruit of the Loom boxers on inside out
beside me, Lori sleeping soundly
her Marvel t-shirt on inside out, too, and backwards
hands tucked under her cheek on the pillow
one thick, muscular thigh draped over my sun-browned leg.

Recalling yesterday afternoon, I smile to myself—
she and I strolling together down the middle of Church
    Street
with a pulsing, writhing mass of bodies
proud and boisterous and brightly dressed (and some not so
    dressed!)
cheering, whistling, shouting, hugging, dancing, singing,
    kissing, frolicking
and how we moved among them, with them
full of abandon and the pleasure of marching together
hands held, eyes wide, and hearts brimming

parading with people who understand the feeling of
living in bodies that were
forbidden to love one another
imperceptible to the rest of the world
scourged, vilified, erased
for so long.

Recalling last night, I smile to myself—
she and I and our lips and collarbones and bellies and thighs
and the heat of our bodies together

made love
made pride
made revolution
made the world.

25
For the land
of Beaver Valley

Lori coaches the girls' snowboard team
at Georgetown High School where she teaches.
She's been coaching this team for many years.
Today, we're up at Beaver Valley Ski Club for the day.
Beaver Valley Ski Club is located in the snow belt,
about an hour and a half north of where Lori and I live.

Her students are competing in some races.
I snowboard a bit now and then and I'm here to help
    chaperone.
It's March 2017.

I have never snowboarded at Beaver Valley before.
I check out their website to learn more about it.
On the homepage of their website it says:

Skiing in the Beaver Valley has been recorded as early as
    February 1936
when the Dominion of Canada Skiing Championships
attracted 20,000 spectators to the valley.
In 1948, the ski site was discovered.

What does it mean when the webpage says,
"The Beaver Valley ski site was "discovered" in 1948"?
What does it mean to name a piece of land in your
    language
when it doesn't belong to you?

They say that Columbus "discovered" America in 1492.
This claim doesn't make sense for two reasons:
First, he didn't discover America because America
    didn't exist in 1492.
Secondly, if they mean he discovered the land, he
    didn't.

Indigenous People have lived on this land, Turtle
    Island—
the land settlers call North America—for thousands of
    years.
Indigenous People have lived in the Beaver Valley for
    thousands of years.
In fact, people have lived on the Niagara Escarpment—
    where the Beaver Valley lies—
for more than 12,000 years.

An article in the Hamilton Spectator on the Niagara Escarpment
that says this:

The Niagara Escarpment has been a bountiful provider of
food, shelter, and resources. Hunters and gatherers arrived
here as the great ice fields retreated at the end of the last
Ice Age, having likely migrated across the Bering land
bridge from Siberia. They were the first known people on the
escarpment at a time when it formed the southern shore of

a great glacial lake that stretched north to the edge of the retreating ice sheet. Favourite camping grounds of these people included the Beaver Valley and particularly Blue Mountain where they harvested Blue Mountain chert, a hard rock similar to flint that they could fashion into spear tips for hunting caribou and mastodon.

When I look up treaty information about the Beaver Valley, I learn that Beaver Valley is part of Treaty No. 18, Lake Simcoe-Nottawasaga.

On the *Indigenous and Northern Affairs* webpage of the *Government of Canada* website, I come across a page titled, "Treaty Texts – Upper Canada Land Surrenders."

I find this information:

Articles of provision agreement entered into on Saturday, the 17th day of October, 1818, between the Honourable William Claus Deputy Superintendent General of Indian Affairs in behalf of His Majesty, of the one part, and Musquakie or Yellow Head, Chief of Rein Deer Tribe, Kaqueticaum, Chief of the Cat Fish Tribe, Maskigonce of the Otter Tribe, Manitobnobe of the Pike Tribe, Principal men of the Chippewa Nation of Indians, inhabiting the northern parts of the unpurchased lands within the Home District, of the other part, Witnesseth: that for and in consideration of the yearly sum of twelve hundred pounds, Province currency, in goods at the Montreal price to be well and tryly paid yearly and every year by His said Majesty to the said Chippewa Nation, inhabiting and claiming the said tract, which may be otherwise known as follows: Bounded by the District of London on the west, by Lake Huron on the north, by the Penetangueshine purchase (made in 1815) on the east, by the south shore of Kempenfelt Bay, the western shore of Lake Simcoe and Cook's Bay and the Holland River to the north-west angle of the Township of King, containing by computation one million, five hundred and ninety-two thousands acres, and the said Musquakie, Kaqueticum, Maskigonce and Monitonobie, as well and for themselves as for the Chippewa Nation inhabiting and claiming the said tract of land as above describe, do freely fully, and voluntarily surrender and convey that same to His Majesty without reservation or limitation in perpetuity.

$1200 pounds worth of goods every year?

In exchange for one million, five-hundred and ninety-two thousand acres in perpetuity?

Goods? Montreal price? What about inflation? The rising cost of living, housing, food, unemployment rates? Urbanization? Gentrification? The loss of land, freedom, life?

Did Indigenous people really "freely, fully, and voluntarily surrender" this land in perpetuity without reservation or limitation?

Regarding the treaties between the Government of Canada and Indigenous Peoples of this land, Michael Asch reminds me "We know full well we have not kept our word. That is a legacy with which we will have to deal, just as we will have to deal with the fact that we violated the principle of temporal priority and settled on lands without first gaining the consent of those already living on them" (Asch, 2014, p. 99).

On the Beaver Valley Ski Club homepage, it also says:

The Davis homestead provided the best prospects for ski terrain and the first tow opened in January 1949. After a decade of financially struggling to operate the hill, an interested group of skiers formed a partnership to operate Beaver Valley Resorts Ltd. Under this group, the resort flourished to include new trails at Lazy Loop and Roller Coaster. The Weber home farm property, which is now the base of the ski club, was acquired, a ski shop and main lodge were erected which created the warm sense of belonging which is hallmark to the Beaver Valley Ski Club today. Now, Beaver Valley is a winter playground, providing members and guests a top-quality skiing experience and a variety of other outdoor activities that are fun for the whole family. Beaver Valley Ski Club is for active families looking to belong to a relaxed and welcoming club where they can spend quality time together and foster new friendships. The club is known for its great terrain park, signature run Avalanche (the steepest groomed run in Ontario with a rich history of daring adventures for great storytelling!) and its friendly atmosphere. Beaver Valley Ski Club provides an attractive and affordable option for private club membership to young families.

There's nothing on the website that talks about
who lived there long before the Davis and Weber families.
There's nothing about it being sacred Indigenous Land

Land on which Indigenous People depended for survival
and spiritual nourishment.
A warm sense of belonging for whom?
Welcoming for what kinds of people?
Fostering new friendships with whom?
The telling stories of whose rich histories and daring
adventures?

It's a private ski club
for those who can afford to pay the one-time initiation
    family fee of $11, 500.00
plus annual membership dues
plus annual capital contribution levies.

At lunch in the cafeteria, people bustle about,
swerving around each other with trays of food,
burgers and French fries, small packets of ketchup and
    mustard
Coke and 7Up in waxed paper cups with clear plastic
    lids and white straws.
A middle-aged couple sits beside me at the table
talking about golfing in the summer and
I think about all the pesticides that leach into golf course
    soils,
chemicals flooding into the streams.
I sit with my lunch I brought from home, surrounded by
    people
but I feel alone here.

After we're done eating, Lori and I put our toques on, zip
    up our coats, put on our gloves,
thump outside in our clunky snowboard boots, and
    grab our boards.
We head over to the chair lift and file into line.

We shimmy up into place as the next chair winds
    around the track
and zooms up behind us.
We sit down and the chair speeds forward out of the
    sheltered chair lift station

whisking us up, up, up into the air, floating
above the trees and over white groomed hills.

It's quiet, except for the whirring and dinging of the chair
as it rumbles over the cogs of each tower we pass
skiers and boarders whizz by down below
scraping across the icy slopes.

We take a selfie on the lift.
Smiling, we have our arms around each other.
I'm happy to be here with Lori.
I think it's cool that she's a snowboard coach
it's kind of hot; I have a thing for jocks.
I twist my body around enough on the chair so I can
    survey the view of
Beaver Valley, the forests, the farmlands, stretching out
    far behind and below us
on this crisp, wintery, sunny day.

At the top of the lift, we arrange our boards
    and bodies,
and glide off the chair and over to one of the runs.
Sitting down beside skiers and boarders, we tighten
    our bindings, stand up, nod to one another, and drop
    down off the lip of the slope.

The wind on my cheeks is bitterly cold as I ride
the snow is slick underneath my board.
Too much rain lately and then temperatures dropping
    sharply overnight
 makes for icy conditions
 I don't feel very confident today.

We carve wide, s-shaped designs in the granular snow
back and forth
back and forth
past rows of trees
over undulating terrain
until we reach the bottom of the hill.

Then, we head over to a nearby run,
where the Georgetown High School girls' team
will be crossing the finish line, along with the other
    racers.
A crowd of people gathers to watch and cheer and
    congratulate the athletes.
The generator that provides electricity
for the loudspeaker and heat for the announcer's hut
growls and vibrates in the background.

The announcer calls out the names, numbers, and
    schools
of each girl who shreds a path around blue and red
    flags
placed in a long curve down slopes covered in snow
made from high-tech machines.

There are 110 girls competing in this race from all over
    Ontario.
I wonder if any of them are Indigenous.
My privileged settler body doesn't always recall
until it recalls
    that I'm surrounded by other privileged settler bodies
    moms, dads, coaches, teachers, students, spectators.

My colonizer/colonized mind forgets
until I remember
that I'm standing on Indigenous land
that we're snowboarding on Indigenous land
that Beaver Valley Ski Club is built on
Anishinabeg and Haudenosaunee land.

26
The summer afternoon

Lori and I ride our bikes through the forest beside the Speed River on our way out to Guelph Lake, a human-made reservoir on the edge of town. Dry pine needles make an orange carpet along the trail. Shafts of sunlight beam through the prickly lodgepole pine boughs overhead. The air is humid and the shade of the trees provides some relief from the July sunshine.

Our bike chains click as they shift over metal sprockets. Twigs snap underneath our tires. We glide through occasional wet patches of mud. The Speed River winds alongside the muddy embankment. Two Mallard ducks stand at the edge of the river and quack to one another. Lori and I pedal alongside one another in silence for a few minutes. But, I want to race. I pump my legs faster. My chest heaves as I zoom ahead.

"Hey!" she calls out from behind me. "You said you wanted to do a mellow ride!"

"I lied!" I yell. "C'mon, put those hockey quads to work!" I laugh, looking back. Lori shakes her head and grins.

I swerve around gnarled trees and manoeuvre over twisted roots. I splash through puddles and duck under low-hanging branches.

"Wahoo!" I holler as I fly down a short hill. I crank my handlebars around a corner and keep pedalling. The forest opens up. The lake appears between the trees.

Lori's voice echoes through the forest. "You suck!"

I turn my head sideways to try and catch a glimpse of her. The trail looks empty. I squeeze the brake levers on my handlebars. My bike comes to a stop at the side of the trail. Putting my feet on the ground, I take the small backpack off my shoulders. I reach inside, pull out my water bottle, and unscrew the lid. I take a swig. My breathing slows. A robin warbles in the branches overhead and a few feet away, a squirrel prattles away on a log. A warm breeze drifts over my bare arms.

Tires and pedals rotate closer and closer on the path behind me. I thrust the water bottle out to Lori as she rides towards me. Jutting my hip out, I give her my cutest grin.

"Water break, sweetheart?"

Her feet push hard against the pedals and she picks up speed again. I see the bulge of muscle in her thighs. Man, I love those quads.

"Water's for losers!" she hollers and speeds past me.

"Dammit!" I jam the lid back on my bottle, stuffing it into my backpack. Slinging the backpack across my shoulders, I jump on my bike, and race to catch up.

When I arrive at our spot overlooking the lake, her bike is leaning against the trunk of a maple tree. She is sprawled on the grass. I park my bike up against hers.

"Water break, sweetheart?" Lori holds out her water bottle. She smirks and raises her eyebrows at me. *Why is she always so cute?*

"You jerk!" I laugh, flopping down beside her.

I put my head on her stomach. Her shirt feels damp and warm. My head moves up and down as her chest expands and falls. Fishing a bandana out of the pocket of my cutoffs, I wipe sweat off my forehead. Lori tucks her hand into the waistband of my shorts. The wind picks up and floats across our sweaty bodies. Sweeping branches of the maple tree sway above us. Pale blue sky peeks between the fluttering leaves. We inhale together. And exhale.

"What kind of bird is that?" Lori asks, pointing past my head towards the trunk of the maple tree. A tiny bird with bluish-grey wings, a caramel-coloured breast, and a black and white striped cap dances up and down the bark.

"Let me check my app!" I retrieve my phone from my pocket and swipe my finger across the front. I click on the red square that says "Audubon Birds," scrolling through the list of "tree-clinging birds," and looking at the tiny photos.

"It's a nuthatch, right?" I show Lori the image of a little bird on my phone.

"Looks like it. What does it sound like, I wonder?" she reaches over and taps the miniature label on the screen that says "songs." Up pops a list of different sounds to pick from. "Toots," "nasal squeaks," and "chattery outbursts" are some of the choices.

She clicks on "toots."

"Yak-yak-yak-yak-yak."

Lori and I look at each other and chuckle. I press it again.

"Yak-yak-yak-yak-yak!"

The nuthatch flits from the trunk over to a branch right above our heads.

"Whoa! Look!" I point.

"I see!" Lori smiles. "Press it again!"

"Yak-yak-yak-yak-yak!"

The nuthatch bobs and skips back and forth along the branch, chirping in response.

"She's singing back to your phone!"

"I know! It's so cool!"

I press "chattery outbursts." A series of trills and tweets erupt from my phone. Another nuthatch darts out from the leaves and lands on another bough above us. And another. And another. And another. They hop and jitter along the tree's limbs. Then, I press "nasal squeaks." Another nuthatch shoots past us and lands on the tree's trunk. He shimmies up and down the bark and cocks his tiny head side to side. He clucks and peeps.

I jab Lori in the hip with my elbow. "There are so many!"

"This is incredible. I've never seen this before," she says.

"Me neither."

A nuthatch rockets down from above and dive-bombs Lori's head, just missing her nose.

"Whoa!" She shrieks and clenches her eyes shut.

It swoops back up into the mass of branches above.

"Wow! Awesome!" I burst out. Grabbing her leg, I laugh with delight.

My heart feels like it's swirling and whirling and filling up with everything. Like it's filling up with all the little nuthatch songs— their chirrups and trills and cheeps. Like it's filling up with the warm wind and the golden late-afternoon sunlight. Like it's filling up with Lori, with us. I get a lump in my throat as I think about how, decades after attending the same high school, our paths crossed again, a few years ago.

I reach over and brush her cheek with my fingertips. She wraps her fingers around mine and brings them to her lips. I roll over and take her body in my arms. We kiss. Her lips feel soft and warm. I rest my cheek on her collarbone. I breathe her in. She smells faintly of men's soap.

Is this what joy feels like?

The tiny birds twitter and frolic and serenade us from above.

We disentangle and lie flat on our backs again, our shoulders touching. As we look up at the sky and watch clouds sail by, the nuthatches dart away, one by one.

Lori turns to me. "Time for dinner?"

"Yeah," I say.

She rolls to her feet and reaches her hand down to help me up. She pulls my body to hers and looks at me.

"Can you feel how much I love you?" she asks, shafts of sunlight streaming down around us.

Tears prickle under my eyelids and I hug her tightly.

"Yeah" I say. "I love you, too."

We hope on our bikes and ride home.

27
Lying on a hill

Do you ever lie down on a hill
and look up at the vast expanse of sky
and thank the universe for helping you escape
an unlivable life?

Do you ever send up prayers of gratitude to the great beyond
for guiding you to this moment—
the moment when you realize
that you have waded alone through the muck
unable to see in the dark of night
yet you moved your body tentatively forward
one foot in front of the other
feeling your way along the walls,
fingers digging into the cracks between the cold stones
searching for something you could cling to—
hoping for something solid to grasp?

Something to steady you as you tread
slowly, fearfully forward
towards a different life—
the life you had once, a long time ago, conjured in your mind
the life you began to breathe into
before you gave it up again
for some fabricated romantic promise of the love of another

or an out-of-body fantasy of security
that slowly faded from view once
you began to awaken to the knowledge that
only you can be responsible
for loving yourself—
only you can be responsible
for pursuing your dreams—
only you can be responsible
for fulfilling your own needs for
joy
solitude
peace
connection
ecstasy?

Your dreams are worth more
than a million unbearable situations.
Your desires are worth as much as
the air that swirls in your lungs
the blood that courses through your veins
your heart that beats out the rhythm of your life
the heat that gathers deep inside you
the tears that move you toward a new beginning.

Forgive yourself.

It is the only door through which love can enter.

Discussion questions and recommended projects

Discussion questions

1. How do the various geographical locations described in the stories influence the author's experiences and identity formation? Can you draw parallels to how place has influenced your own identity?

2. In what ways do the stories illustrate the concept of intersectionality? How do multiple aspects of the author's identity interact and affect their experiences?

3. What coping mechanisms and forms of resilience does the author describe in navigating queerphobia, trauma, and other challenges? How do these strategies compare to those discussed in academic literature?

4. How do relationships and community play a role in the author's journey of self-discovery and acceptance? What are the impacts of community support, or lack thereof, in the stories?

5. How does the author portray family relationships and their impact on their identity and well-being? In what ways do

these family dynamics align with or differ from those in your own life or other literature you've read?

6. Despite the challenges faced, the author also writes about joy and love. How are these positive experiences depicted, and what significance do they hold in the overall narrative?

7. How did the stories resonate with your own experiences or challenge your preconceptions? What emotions or thoughts did they evoke, and why?

8. How do the personal narratives in the book enhance your understanding of the academic texts you've studied? Can you identify specific theories or research findings that are illustrated by the author's experiences?

Projects

1. Keep a reflective journal throughout the course, documenting personal responses to the book and related academic readings. Journals should focus on how the personal narratives deepen readers' understanding of the research and how their perspectives evolve over time. The final journal should include a summary of key insights and reflections.

2. Conduct a qualitative research project where you interview members of the LGBTQ+ community about their experiences related to identity, place, and intersectionality. The project should include a literature review, methodology, analysis of the interviews, and a discussion of how the findings relate to the themes in the book and existing research.

3. Produce a piece of creative work (e.g., a short story, poem, visual art, or performance) that explores themes from the book. Creative work(s) will be accompanied by an essay that explains the inspiration behind your work, how it connects to the book's themes, and its relevance to the academic concepts discussed in the course.

Notes

1. The town of Ayr and the surrounding farmland is located on the Haldimand Tract of the Six Nations—Mohawk, Seneca, Oneida, Cayuga, Onondaga and Tuscarora.

2. Canmore and Banff are located on Treaty 7 and the traditional lands of the Blackfoot Confederacy, the Stoney Nakoda, and the Tsuut'ina First Nations. Vancouver is located on the traditional, ancestral, unceded, and occupied territories of three Coast Salish nations: the Skwxwú7mesh, Tsliel-wahtuth, and Xméthkwyiem.

3. RCMP stands for "Royal Canadian Mounted Police," or, more colloquially, "the Mounties." The RCMP is the national police service of Canada.

4. Reid, K. (2011). *Heal myself* [Song]. On *Comin' alive*. Kael Reid Music. https://kaelreid.com/music

5. Reid, K. (2011). *Truckdriver* [Song]. On *I'm just warming up*. Kael Reid Music. https://kaelreid.com/music

6. Reid, K. (2011). *The only dyke at the open mic* [Song]. On *I'm just warming up*. Kael Reid Music. https://kaelreid.com/music

7. Reid, K. (2011). *Crying holy* [Song]. On *Doing it for the chicks*. Kael Reid Music. https://kaelreid.com/music

8. Reid, K. (2011). *When I was a little boy* [Song]. On *Doing it for the chicks*. Kael Reid Music. https://kaelreid.com/music

9. Reid, K. (2019). *Something 'bout you and me* [Song, single]. Kael Reid Music. https://kaelreid.com/music

References

Asch, M. (2014). *On Being Here to Stay: Treaties and Aboriginal Rights in Canada*. Toronto: University of Toronto Press.

Avery, R. (2008). A iker's haven in Beaver Valley: The quest for the dream began with a handshake. *The Star*. [online] Available at: www.thestar.com/life/travel/2008/10/16/a-hikers-haven-in-beaver-valley.html [Accessed 31 Jul. 2024].

Beaver Valley Ski Club. (n.d.). [online] Available at: www.beaverval ley.ca [Accessed 31 Jul. 2024].

Cliff, J. (1972). You Can Get It If You Really Want. [Song] On *The Harder They Come*. US: Mango Records.

Collins, P. (1988). Two Hearts. [Song] On *Buster: The Original Motion Picture Soundtrack*. US: Atlantic Records.

Drumke, M. (1994). Someone. [Song] On *Go Fish Original Motion Picture Soundtrack*. US: Samuel Goldwyn Company.

Ellen. (1997). *The Puppy Episode*. [Television] US: ABC.

Fine Young Cannibals. (1988). She Drives Me Crazy. [Song] On *The Raw & the Cooked*. UK: London Records.

First Nations and Treaties. (n.d.). [online] Available at: www.files. ontario.ca [Accessed 31 Jul. 2024].

Government of Canada. (n.d.). Treaty Texts – Upper Canada Land Surrenders. [online] Available at: www.aadnc-aandc.ca/eng/1370372152585/1370372222012#ucls16 [Accessed 31 Jul. 2024].

Hamilton Spectator. (2005). *The Niagara Escarpment*. [online] Available at: www.beavervalley.ca/discover-the-club/ [Accessed 31 Jul. 2024].

Hoff, B. (1982). *The Tao of Pooh*. New York, NY: Dutton.

Madonna. (1989). Like a Prayer. [Song] On *Like a Prayer*. US: Sire Records.

Reid, K. (2006). Heal Myself. [Song] On *Comin' Alive*. Canada: Independent.

Reid, K. (2009). The Only Dyke at the Open Mic [Song] On *I'm Just Warming Up*. Canada: Independent.

Reid, K. (2009). Truckdriver. [Song] On *I'm Just Warming Up*. Canada: Independent.

Reid, K. (2011). Crying Holy. [Song] On *Doing it for the Chicks*. Canada: Independent.

Reid, K. (2011). When I was a Little Boy. [Song] On *Doing it for the Chicks*. Canada: Independent.

Reid, K. (2016). Something 'Bout You and Me. [Song]. https://kaelreid.com/music/

Rich, A. (1980). Compulsory Heterosexuality and Lesbian Existence. *Signs*, 5(4), pp. 631–660.

Swift, E. (2002). Include My Food. [Song] On *Stiltwalking*. Canada: Few'll Ignite Sound.

Troche, R. (Director). (1994). *Go Fish*. [Film] USA: Samuel Goldwyn Company.

Vere, T. (n.d.). G-String. [Song] On *Just to Be*. Canada: Independent.

Wikipedia. (n.d.). *Kawartha Lakes*. [online] Available at: https://en.wikipedia.org/wiki/Kawartha_Lakes [Accessed 31 Jul. 2024].

Recommended resources

Ahmed, S. (2006). *Queer Phenomenology: Orientations, Objects, Others*. Durham, NC: Duke University Press.

Anzaldua, G. (1987). *Borderlands/La Frontera*. San Francisco, SF: Aunt Lute Books.

Belcourt, B. (2022). *A History of My Brief Body*. New York, NY: Hamish Hamilton.

Bornstein, K, & Bergman, S. B. eds. (2010). *Gender Outlaws: The Next Generation*. Berkeley, CA: Seal Press.

Dawson, J. (2014). *This Book is Gay*. Naperville, NV: Sourcebooks Fire.

Dykewomon, E. (1997). *Beyond the Pale*. Vancouver: Raincoast Books.

Feinberg, L. (1993). *Stone Butch Blues*. Ithaca, NY: Firebrand Books.

Gajdics, P. (2017). *The Inheritance of Shame: A Memoir*. Long Beach, CA: Brown Paper Press.

Lorde, A. (1984). *Sister Outsider*. Berkeley, CA: Ten Speed Press.

Oliver, M. (1992). *The Summer's Day*. In *New and Selected Poems, Volume One*. Boston, BO: Beacon Press, p. 94.

Oliver, M. (1986). *Wild Geese*. In *Dream Work*. Boston, BO: Atlantic Monthly Press, p. 14.

Reid, K. (2006). Heal Myself. [Song] In *Comin' Alive*. Self-released. Spotify.

Reid, K. (2009). The Only Dyke at the Open Mic. [Song] In *I'm Just Warming Up*. Self-released. Spotify.

Reid, K. (2009). Truckdriver. [Song] In *I'm Just Warming Up*. Self-released. Spotify.

Reid, K. (2011). Crying Holy. [Song] In *Doing it for the Chicks*. Self-released. Spotify.

Reid, K. (2011). Doing it for the Chicks. [Song] In *Doing it for the Chicks*. Self-released. Spotify.

Reid, K. (2011). When I was a Little Boy. [Song] In *Doing it for the Chicks*. Self-released. Spotify.

Shraya, V. (2018). *I'm Afraid of Men*. Toronto: Penguin Canada.

Walker, A. (2003). SM. In *Absolute Trust in the Goodness of the Earth: New Poems*. New York, NY: Random House.

Whitehead, J. (2018). *Jonny Appleseed*. Vancouver: Arsenal Pulp Press.

Index

bodies. 1, 189, 190, 199, 200; and abortion. 103, 108, 111; and anger. 154; and assault. 33–38, 39; and attraction. 9, 10, 13, 18, 24, 26, 28, 42, 91, 93, 98, 165, 167, 181, 182, 194, 195, 197; and gender. 12, 18, 173–80; and illness. 141, 142, 146; and land. 67, 127, 162–63; and sex. 95; and sexuality. 63, 67, 104, 111, 147; and substance use. 33, 49, 50, 51, 52, 53, 54, 55, 56, 57; in public. 24, 26, 28, 137, 141

feminism. 64, 96, 150, 175

flesh. 28, 34, 55, 63, 153, 174

gender. 5, 6, 23, 35, 43, 44, 47, 48, 114, 159–60; and feminism. 150; and men. 61, 96, 135; and sexuality. 104, 139; and violence. 101; and women. 113, 121, 134; diversity. 173–80

homophobia. 71, 72, 73, 75, 77, 78, 79–89, 93, 114, 125, 147

identities. 53; and gender. 5, 159–60, 175, 176, 178, 180; and queerness. 1, 102, 136, 144, 146, 150, 151, 161–62

kissing. 16, 17, 33, 54, 75, 102, 181, 197

land. 54, 55, 57, 58, 86, 123, 142, 147, 189; and adolescence. 23; and anger. 156, 157; and bodies. 36–37, 39, 67; and childhood. 3–5, 6–8, 115, 166, 167; and leaving. 161–63; and songs. 113, 114; and teaching. 97; enjoyment of. 69, 73, 126–29, 141, 173, 181, 193–97, 199; Indigenous. 183–87, 190; living on. 91, 99, 103, 105, 106, 107, 109, 111

lesbians. 63–65, 67, 74, 76, 77, 78, 80, 81, 82, 92, 93, 96, 102, 104, 111, 133, 143, 150–51, 162; and adolescence. 17; and shows. 133–39; and songs. 119–21, 125

love. 37, 55, 70, 71, 103, 106, 114, 162, 166, 198, 199–200; and family. 92; and land. 163; and queerness. 2, 64, 67, 75, 96, 111, 147, 150, 182, 194; *and songs*. 28, 121, 137; self-. 114

music. 73, 89; at venues. 24, 26, 27, 28, 29, 55, 133; listening to. 42, 43, 48, 49, 52, 62, 64, 94, 110, 116, 119; performing.

119–21, 123, 124, 128, 133–39, 149, 150; playing. 54

place. 2, 8, 46, 92, 93, 97, 105, 114, 116, 127, 132, 134, 136, 137, 162, 167

relationships. 1–3, 102, 127, 149; and bodies. 179; and boyfriends. 12, 42–59, 61, 62, 91–98, 103, 107, 109, 111; and family. 4, 5, 7–8, 23, 71, 75, 79–89, 113, 141–47, 149, 160; and friendships. 9–19, 99, 107, 108, 133, 149, 150, 151, 187; and girlfriends. 67–90, 171, 193–98; and songs. 116

sex. 182; and adolescence. 16–18, 23, 49; and assault. 61–62, 114, 154–58; and boyfriends. 61–62; and porn. 18, 63–65, 94–97; and pregnancy. 100–2; and substance use. 53

sexuality. 53, 63, 93, 104, 174; and publicness. 75–78, 82, 92, 93, 120, 142–46, 149–51

songs. 110, 113, 115–19, 132, 159–60, 195, 196, 197; and land. 163; performing. 137, 138, 139

songwriting. 62, 110, 124, 128, 129, 133, 149

spirit. 8, 103, 129, 167, 187

storytelling. 1–2, 26, 114, 128, 161, 167, 187

substance use. 10, 12, 18, 23, 25–32, 47–56, 58, 73, 76, 80, 82, 83, 93, 94, 116, 120, 138, 139

teaching. 10–12, 43, 54, 70, 78, 82, 87, 89, 91, 92, 93, 94, 183

transgender people. 143, 173–80

www.ingramcontent.com/pod-product-compliance
Lightning Source LLC
Chambersburg PA
CBHW070325270326
41926CB00017B/3768